FOOD LOVERS

CHICKEN

RECIPES SELECTED BY JONNIE LEGÉR

Trans
Atlantic
Press

All recipes serve four people, unless otherwise indicated.

For best results when cooking the recipes in this book, buy fresh ingredients and follow the instructions carefully. Make sure that everything is properly cooked through before serving, particularly any meat and shellfish, and note that as a general rule vulnerable groups such as the very young, elderly people and pregnant women should avoid dishes that contain raw eggs. Take care when cooking with chilies, If slicing or chopping chilies, it is a wise precaution to wear disposable plastic gloves. Take care not to touch your eyes if you have been handling chilies.

For all recipes, quantities are given in standard U.S. cups and imperial measures, followed by the metric equivalent. Follow one set or the other, but not a mixture of both because conversions may not be exact. Standard spoon and cup measurements are level and are based on the following:

1 tsp = 5 ml, 1 tbsp = 15 ml, 1 cup = 250 ml / 8 fl oz.

Note that Australian standard tablespoons are 20 ml, so Australian readers should use 3 tsp in place of 1 tbsp when measuring small quantities.

The electric oven temperatures in this book are given for conventional ovens with top and bottom heat. When using a fan oven, the temperature should be decreased by about 20–40ºF / 10–20ºC – check the oven manufacturer's instruction book for further guidance.

3 tbsp tomato paste (purée)

¼ tsp cayenne pepper

Salt and pepper

3 small potatoes, roughly chopped

1 onion, sliced

14 oz / 400 g can chopped tomatoes

1 cup / 75 g fresh or frozen lima
(butter) beans

1 tbsp Worcestershire sauce

½ cup / 125 ml water

14 oz / 400 g can sweetcorn kernels,
drained

minutes.

2. Remove the chicken thighs from the pan
and cut the meat away from the bones.
Shred the chicken, discard the bones and
return the chicken to the pan.

3. Add the potatoes, onions, tomatoes, lima
(butter) beans and Worcestershire sauce.
Cover the pan and simmer for 1 hour,
stirring occasionally.

4. Add the water and sweetcorn, stirring
to prevent it from scorching, simmer for a
further 20 minutes and serve.

SOUPS, STARTERS AND SNACKS

CHICKEN NOODLE SOUP

Ingredients

1 chicken, weighing about
3 lb 8 oz / 1.6 kg

1 inch / 2.5 cm piece fresh ginger,
sliced

1 tbsp tomato paste

Salt and pepper

1 garlic clove

2 carrots, roughly chopped

2 parsnips, roughly chopped

1 celery stalk, roughly chopped

1 onion, roughly chopped

4 scallions (spring onions), sliced

2 red chilies, finely chopped and
deseeded

3–4 oz / 100 g fine noodles

2 cups / 50 g fresh cilantro
(coriander) leaves

Method

Prep and cook time: 1 hour 20 min

1. Put the chicken in a large saucepan with
enough cold water to cover. Bring to a boil
and when the water boils, skim off any scum
that rises to the surface.

2. Add the ginger to the pan with the tomato
paste, salt, pepper, garlic, carrots, parsnips,
celery and onion. Simmer over a low heat,
partially covered, for about 45–60 minutes
until the chicken is tender and cooked
through.

3. Remove the chicken from the pan. Strain
the broth (stock) and return it to the pan,
discarding the vegetables. Keep warm.

4. Put the noodles into a separate pan with
some of the broth and cook according to the
packet instructions until tender but still with
a slight bite. Keep warm.

5. Remove the skin from the chicken, pull
the meat from the bones and chop the meat
into bite-size pieces.

6. To serve, put the meat and noodles into
4 serving bowls and sprinkle on the scallions
and chopped chilies. Pour over the hot
broth and garnish with the chopped cilantro
(coriander).

CONTENTS

SOUPS, STARTERS AND SNACKS

CHICKEN NOODLE SOUP

Ingredients

1 chicken, weighing about
3 lb 8 oz / 1.6 kg

1 inch / 2.5 cm piece fresh ginger,
sliced

1 tbsp tomato paste

Salt and pepper

1 garlic clove

2 carrots, roughly chopped

2 parsnips, roughly chopped

1 celery stalk, roughly chopped

1 onion, roughly chopped

4 scallions (spring onions), sliced

2 red chilies, finely chopped and
deseeded

3–4 oz / 100 g fine noodles

2 cups / 50 g fresh cilantro
(coriander) leaves

Method

Prep and cook time: 1 hour 20 min

1. Put the chicken in a large saucepan with
enough cold water to cover. Bring to a boil
and when the water boils, skim off any scum
that rises to the surface.

2. Add the ginger to the pan with the tomato
paste, salt, pepper, garlic, carrots, parsnips,
celery and onion. Simmer over a low heat,
partially covered, for about 45–60 minutes
until the chicken is tender and cooked
through.

3. Remove the chicken from the pan. Strain
the broth (stock) and return it to the pan,
discarding the vegetables. Keep warm.

4. Put the noodles into a separate pan with
some of the broth and cook according to the
packet instructions until tender but still with
a slight bite. Keep warm.

5. Remove the skin from the chicken, pull
the meat from the bones and chop the meat
into bite-size pieces.

6. To serve, put the meat and noodles into
4 serving bowls and sprinkle on the scallions
and chopped chilies. Pour over the hot
broth and garnish with the chopped cilantro
(coriander).

KENTUCKY BURGOO SOUP

Ingredients

1 lb / 450 g chicken thighs, skinned

8 oz / 225 g stewing steak, cubed

3 cups / 750 ml chicken broth (stock)

3 tbsp tomato paste (purée)

¼ tsp cayenne pepper

Salt and pepper

3 small potatoes, roughly chopped

1 onion, sliced

14 oz / 400 g can chopped tomatoes

1 cup / 75 g fresh or frozen lima
(butter) beans

1 tbsp Worcestershire sauce

½ cup / 125 ml water

14 oz / 400 g can sweetcorn kernels,
drained

Method

Prep and cook time: 2 hours

1. Put the chicken, beef, broth (stock),
tomato paste (purée) and cayenne
pepper into a large saucepan. Season
generously with salt and pepper. Simmer
for 30 minutes.

2. Remove the chicken thighs from the pan
and cut the meat away from the bones.
Shred the chicken, discard the bones and
return the chicken to the pan.

3. Add the potatoes, onions, tomatoes, lima
(butter) beans and Worcestershire sauce.
Cover the pan and simmer for 1 hour,
stirring occasionally.

4. Add the water and sweetcorn, stirring
to prevent it from scorching, simmer for a
further 20 minutes and serve.

CREAMY CHOWDER

Ingredient

2 tbsp oil

3 potatoes, peeled and diced

1 red bell pepper, diced

1 onion, diced

3½ cups / 800 ml chicken broth (stock)

1 lb / 450 g frozen corn kernels, thawed

8 oz / 250 g cooked chicken

7 tbsp / 100 ml cream

Salt and pepper

1 sprig rosemary, to garnish

Method

Prep and cook time: 30 mins

1. Heat the oil in a pan, then cook the potatoes, bell pepper and onion for 5 minutes.

2. Stir in the broth (stock), bring to a boil and simmer for 15 minutes.

3. Add the corn to the pan and cook for 3 minutes. Stir in the cooked chicken and the cream and reheat until piping hot. Season to taste with salt and pepper and garnish with a sprig of rosemary.

CHICKEN AND TOFU SOUP

Ingredients

1 tbsp vegetable oil

2 carrots, diced

4 scallions (spring onions), green parts sliced into strips

1¾ cups / 400 ml coconut milk

1–2 tsp grated fresh ginger

2 cups / 475 ml water

2 boneless chicken breasts, skinned and chopped into cubes

8 oz / 225 g tofu, cubed

4 oz / 120 g snow (sugar snap) peas

4 tbsp fish sauce

4 tbsp lime juice

Salt

Sugar

1 tbsp chopped fresh cilantro (coriander) leaves

Method

Prep and cook time: 35 min

1. Heat the oil in a large saucepan. Add the carrots and chopped scallions (spring onions) and fry for 2–3 minutes.

2. Add the coconut milk, ginger and water and bring to the boil.

3. Add the chicken, tofu and snow (sugar snap) peas. Stir in the fish sauce and lime juice. Simmer for about 15 minutes, until the chicken is thoroughly cooked through.

4. Season with salt and sugar to taste. Stir in the cilantro (coriander) leaves.

5. Serve the soup garnished with the scallion strips.

CURRIED CHICKEN AND POTATO SOUP

Ingredients

2–3 large boiling potatoes

2 large carrots

1 onion

2 chicken breasts

2 tbsp oil

Salt and pepper

1 tbsp curry powder

½ tsp cinnamon

2 tsp garam masala

4½ cups / 600 ml chicken or vegetable broth (stock)

1¼ cups / 300 g yogurt

3 tbsp mint leaves, chopped

Salt & freshly milled pepper

Method

Prep and cook time: 20 min

1. Peel the potatoes, then rinse and dice. Peel the carrots, cut in half lengthways, then cut diagonally. Peel the onion and cut into slices.

2. Cut the chicken into bite-size pieces and fry in hot oil. Season to taste with salt, pepper and curry powder. Take out of the skillet (frying pan).

3. Sauté the potatoes, carrots and onions in the meat fat, stirring continually. Season to taste with salt and pepper. Stir in the rest of the spices and pour in the vegetable broth (stock). Simmer gently for about 10 minutes. Add the chicken pieces and simmer for a further 4–5 minutes. Season to taste.

4. Mix the yogurt with 2 tablespoons of chopped mint.

5. Pour the soup into serving bowls and garnish with a spoonful of yogurt sauce and some chopped mint.

NOODLE SOUP WITH CHICKEN AND NUTS

Ingredients

4 cups / 1 liter vegetable broth (stock)

1 stick lemongrass

4 tbsp light soy sauce

3 tbsp lime juice

½ inch / 1 cm ginger, chopped

1 clove garlic, chopped

8 oz / 250 g chicken breast

1 red chili, sliced into rings

1 cup / 120 g snow peas (mangetout), thinly sliced

2 tomatoes, deseeded and cut into thin slices

2 Chinese cabbage leaves, sliced into strips

7oz / 200 g Asian egg noodles

¾ cup / 40 g walnuts, roughly chopped

1 bunch fresh cilantro (coriander)

Method

Prep and cook time: 25 min

1. Put the vegetable broth (stock), lemongrass, 2 tablespoons of soy sauce, 2 tablespoons of lime juice, the ginger and garlic in a saucepan and bring to a boil. Now add the chicken breast, cover with a lid and simmer for about 15 minutes over a low to medium heat.

2. Add the vegetables to the soup.

3. Remove the lemongrass and the chicken breast from the broth. Cut the meat into bite-size pieces.

4. Put the noodles in the soup and simmer for about 2 minutes in the broth. Add the meat and warm. Season with soy sauce and lime juice. Garnish with the roughly chopped walnuts and cilantro (coriander) leaves before serving.

LENTIL SOUP WITH CHICKEN AND BALSAMIC ONIONS

Ingredients

5 tbsp / 75 g butter

1 onion, finely diced

1 clove garlic, peeled

1 tsp ground coriander

1 lb 2 oz / 450 g sweet potatoes, peeled and chopped

1 leek, trimmed and sliced

4 cups / 1 liter vegetable broth (stock)

½ cup /100 g red lentils

8 oz / 250 g cooked chicken, shredded

2 red onions, sliced

4 tbsp balsamic vinegar

Salt & freshly milled pepper

2 tbsp snipped chives

Method

Prep and cook time: 1 hour

1. Heat the 3 tbsp (45 g) of the butter and sauté the onion until translucent, press in the garlic and sauté briefly. Stir in the coriander, then add the sweet potatoes and leek and sauté, stirring, for about 5 minutes.

2 Pour in the vegetable broth (stock) and the lentils, cover and simmer for about 30 minutes. Add the shredded cooked chicken a few minutes before the end of the cooking time.

3. Meanwhile, prepare the balsamic onions. Sauté the red onions in the remaining butter until soft. Add the balsamic vinegar and simmer until slightly reduced.

4. Remove the soup from the heat, season to taste with salt and pepper, stir in the chives and ladle into plates or bowls. Serve garnished with a spoonful of balsamic onions.

WHITE BEAN, CHICKEN AND CARROT SOUP

Ingredients

1¼ cups /250 g dried white beans

5 cups /1¼ litres cold water

1 tbsp olive oil

1 onion, finely chopped

4 cloves garlic, finely chopped

1 large potato, peeled and diced

1 fennel bulb, trimmed and chopped

2 large carrots, diced

8 oz / 250 g cooked chicken, finely chopped

2 tsp chopped fresh sage leaves, plus some whole leaves for garnish

1 tsp chopped fresh rosemary leaves

Salt & freshly milled pepper

1 tbsp grated Parmesan cheese

Method

Prep and cook time: 1 h 30 min plus 12 hours soaking time

1. Put the beans in a bowl, cover with water and soak overnight.

2. Drain the beans. Add them to the cold water, bring to a boil, then simmer for about 1 hour.

3. Fry the onions and the garlic in hot oil until soft. Add the potatoes, fennel and carrots and sauté. Then add to the beans and cooked chicken and simmer for 20 minutes. Sprinkle in the chopped sage leaves and rosemary leaves and season with salt and pepper.

4. Stir in the grated Parmesan cheese. Garnish with a few sage leaves and serve.

CHICKEN SOUP WITH POTATO DUMPLINGS

Ingredients

For the dumplings:

1 lb 12 oz / 800 g baking potatoes

1 egg

3–4 tbsp potato starch

3 tbsp snipped chives

For the soup:

9 oz / 250 g carrots, thinly sliced

3 stalks celery, thinly sliced

I head of broccoli, cut into small florets

2 tbsp olive oil

2 sprigs rosemary

6 cups / 1½ liters chicken broth (stock)

1 skinless, boneless chicken breast, chopped

1/3 cup / 50 g frozen peas

Salt & freshly milled pepper

3 tbsp snipped chives

Grated Parmesan cheese

Method

Prep and cook time: 1 hour 15 min

1. For the dumplings, steam half of the potatoes for about 30 minutes, until cooked. Peel and press through a potato ricer. Peel the rest of the potatoes, grate finely and add to the cooked potatoes. Stir in the egg and chives. Season with salt and add enough potato starch to produce a shapeable 'dough'. Cook a test dumpling in hot water. Then, with moistened hands form into about 20 small dumplings. Cook very gently in simmering, salted water for about 20 minutes.

2. Meanwhile, heat the oil in a pan and sauté the prepared vegetables (apart from the peas). Add the rosemary sprigs, the broth (stock) and the chicken breast, bring to a boil and simmer for about 15 minutes until everything is cooked. Add the peas after 5 minutes.

3. Season the soup to taste with salt and pepper. Put the drained dumplings and the rest of the chives into the soup, ladle into bowls and serve sprinkled with Parmesan cheese.

LEMON CHICKEN SOUP

Ingredients

4 stalks lemongrass, peeled and cut into thin strips lengthways

2 kaffir lime leaves, roughly chopped

2 oz / 50 g galangal, peeled and thinly sliced crossways

2 oz / 50 g ginger, peeled and thinly sliced crossways

1 red chili, deseeded and finely chopped

6 cups / 1¼ liters chicken broth (stock)

14 oz / 400 g chicken breast fillet

About 4 oz / 120 g chestnut mushrooms (brown button mushrooms), sliced

5–6 oz / 160 g shiitake mushrooms, sliced

4 tbsp lemon juice

4 tbsp fish sauce

Salt & freshly ground black pepper

Cilantro (coriander) leaves

Method

Prep and cook time: 35 min

1. Put the lemongrass, kaffir lime leaves, galangal, ginger and chili into a pan with the chicken broth (stock), bring to a boil and simmer for 12 minutes.

2. Add the chicken breast and simmer for a further 5 minutes. Then remove the chicken breast from the soup and cut into strips crossways.

3. Return the sliced chicken to the broth along with the mushrooms and cook very gently for 4 minutes. Add lemon juice, fish sauce, salt and pepper to taste. Sprinkle with cilantro (coriander) leaves before serving.

CHICKEN AND RICE NOODLE SOUP

Ingredients

10 oz / 300 g chicken breast, cut into bite-size pieces

1 tbsp cornstarch (cornflour)

2 tbsp sesame oil

1 clove garlic, finely chopped

½ inch / 1 cm piece ginger, peeled and finely chopped

1 tsp curcuma (turmeric)

4 cups / 1 liter vegetable broth (stock)

1 stick lemongrass, cut into strips

7 oz / 200 g rice noodles

4 scallions (spring onions), cut into rings, plus some strips for garnish

1 small Napa cabbage (Chinese leaves), chopped

8 cherry tomatoes, quartered

2 tomatoes, diced

4 tbsp light soy sauce

4 tbsp lime juice

Thai basil, to garnish

Method

Prep and cook time: 25 min

1. Mix the chicken pieces and the cornstarch (cornflour) in a bowl.

2. Heat the sesame oil in a saucepan and fry the chicken until lightly browned. Add the garlic, ginger, and curcuma (turmeric) and sauté, then pour in the vegetable broth (stock) and bring to a boil.

3. Add the lemongrass to the soup and simmer for about 5 minutes.

4. Put the rice noodles in the soup and simmer for a further 1–2 minutes over a low heat. Add the Napa cabbage (Chinese leaves), scallions (spring onions), cherry tomatoes, and tomatoes and warm thoroughly.

5. Season to taste with soy sauce and lime juice. Garnish with Thai basil and scallion strips and serve.

CURRIED CHICKEN SOUP WITH GINGER

Ingredients

2 tbsp oil

2 chicken breast fillets, cut into strips

2 tsp yellow curry paste

3 garlic cloves, peeled and chopped

2 tsp freshly grated ginger root

1 tsp ground coriander

1 tsp curcuma (turmeric)

1 tsp sugar

½ tsp grated lemon zest

3–4 tbsp lemon juice

1 tbsp fish sauce

3 shallots, thinly sliced

4 cups / 1 liter chicken broth (stock)

1¾ cups / 400 ml coconut milk, unsweetened

7 oz / 200 g fresh Chinese egg noodles

1 cup / 100 g bean sprouts

Cucumber slices and mint leaves, to garnish

Method

Prep and cook time: 30 min

1. Heat the oil in a large pan. Sauté the chicken, stirring, for about 4 minutes. Add the curry paste, garlic, ginger, coriander, curcuma (turmeric), sugar and lemon zest and cook for 3–4 minutes, stirring constantly.

2. Add the lemon juice, fish sauce, sliced shallots, chicken broth (stock) and coconut milk, bring to a boil and simmer, uncovered, for about 15 minutes.

3. Meanwhile, cook the noodles in a pan of water for 5–7 minutes, or until soft, drain through a sieve.

4. Put the noodles in bowls and fill up with soup. Garnish with bean sprouts, cucumber slices and mint leaves and serve immediately.

SWISS BARLEY SOUP

Ingredients

1 tbsp butter

2 carrots, peeled and finely diced

¾ cup / 125 g celery root (celeriac), peeled and finely chopped

2 potatoes, peeled and finely chopped

2 leeks, finely sliced

4–5 Savoy cabbage leaves, finely sliced, plus some to garnish

Scant ½ cup / 80 g barley

1 onion

1 bay leaf

1 clove

8 cups / 2 liters chicken broth (stock)

Salt & freshly milled pepper

Approx 12 oz / 350 g chicken legs or thighs

4 oz / 125 g smoked bacon, chopped

4 oz / 125 g smoked pork, chopped into bite-size pieces

Method

Prep and cook time: 2 hours 20 min

1. Heat the butter in a large saucepan. Fry the vegetables in the butter, add the barley and sauté.

2. Meanwhile, peel the onion and push the clove and bay leaf into it.

3. Pour in the chicken broth (stock) into the vegetables and season with salt and pepper. Add the onion, chicken, bacon and pork, cover and simmer for about 2 hours.

4. Remove the chicken and onion from the pan. Cut the chicken meat away from the bone and return the meat to the soup. Discard the onion.

5. Season to taste and serve garnished with strips of Savoy cabbage.

THAI TOM YUM SOUP

Ingredients

2 chicken legs

2 red chili peppers, cut into rings

10 oz / 300 g string beans, trimmed

4 cups / 1 litre beef broth (stock)

2 kaffir lime leaves

1 stalk lemongrass, slightly crushed

1 tsp ginger, freshly grated

1 tsp tamarind concentrate

10 oz / 300 g mini corns

Fish sauce

Chili sauce

Soybean sprouts, to garnish

Method

Prep and cook time: 25 min

1. Remove the skin from the chicken, remove the bone and cut into bite-size pieces.

2. Bring the beef broth (stock), kaffir lime leaves, the lemongrass, ginger and tamarind concentrate to a boil. Add the string beans and simmer gently for about 2–3 minutes. Add the chicken, chili and mini corns and simmer for another 5–6 minutes or until the chicken is cooked.

3. Season with fish sauce and chili sauce. Remove the lemongrass stick, garnish with the soybean sprouts and serve.

SPICY PEA SOUP WITH CHICKEN AND VEGETABLES

Ingredients

²/₃ cup / 100 g brown dried peas

Olive oil

1 tsp cumin seed

3 garlic cloves, finely chopped

4 scallions (spring onions), chopped

2 tsp grated ginger

2 tsp garam masala

2–3 green chilies, deseeded and finely chopped

14 oz / 400 g cauliflower, divided into small florets

14 oz / 400 g pumpkin, diced

3 cups / 750 ml water

1 tsp tomato paste (purée)

Salt

10 oz / 300 g cooked chicken, cut into bite-size pieces

8 tbsp sour cream, to garnish

Method

Prep and cook time: 1 hour plus 12 hours soaking time

1. Soak the peas in water overnight.

2. Drain and rinse the peas. Heat 4–5 tablespoons oil in a wide pan and briefly sauté the cumin seeds. Add the garlic, scallions (spring onions), ginger, garam masala and chili and sauté briefly.

3. Add the pumpkin and cauliflower, sauté briefly, then pour in the water. Stir in the tomato paste (purée) and peas and season with 1–2 teaspoons salt and bring to a boil. Then reduce the heat, add the cooked chicken and cover and simmer over a low heat for 30–35 minutes.

4. Season to taste with salt. Ladle into soup bowls and serve. Add a little sour cream to each bowl, if desired.

THAI CHICKEN SOUP WITH COCONUT MILK

Ingredients

14 oz / about 400 g chicken breast

1 cup / 100 g oyster mushrooms

2 medium sized tomatoes

1 red chili

1¾ cups / 400 ml canned coconut milk, unsweetened

2¼ cups / 600 ml water

1–2 tsp freshly grated ginger

4 tbsp fish sauce

4 tbsp lime juice

Sugar

Salt

1 tbsp freshly copped cilantro (coriander)

Method
Prep and cook time: 35 min

1. Cut the chicken breasts into bite-size pieces. Clean the oyster mushrooms and slice. Quarter, de-seed and chop the tomatoes. Cut the chili in half lengthways, de-seed and finely chop.

2. Heat the coconut milk in a pan together with the water and bring to a boil.

3. Add the chicken, mushrooms, tomatoes, ginger and chili and season to taste with fish sauce and lime juice. Simmer for about 5 minutes or until the chicken is cooked through. Add sugar and salt to taste and sprinkle chopped cilantro (coriander) over the top and serve.

BROCCOLI SOUP WITH CHICKEN AND CORN

Ingredients

3 tbsp butter

1 onion, finely chopped

3 cloves garlic, finely chopped

7 oz / 200 g button mushrooms, sliced

1 head of broccoli, cut into small florets

3¼ cups / 800 ml chicken or vegetable broth (stock)

1 tbsp flour

Scant ½ cup / 100 g whipping cream

10 oz / 300 g can of corn kernels, drained

8 oz / 250 g cooked chicken

Salt & freshly milled pepper

1 tbsp finely chopped parsley leaves

Method

Prep and cook time: 35 min

1. Heat 2 tablespoons of the butter in a pan and sauté the onion and garlic until translucent. Add the mushrooms and broccoli and sauté all together. Pour in the broth (stock) and bring to a boil. Reduce the heat, cover and simmer for 15 minutes.

2. Blend together the remaining butter and the flour and stir the paste into the soup. Stir in the cream, corn kernels and cooked chicken and briefly bring to a boil.

3. Season with salt and pepper and garnish with chopped parsley leaves.

CHICKEN SOUP WITH ALMONDS

Ingredients

4 tbsp sunflower oil

4 chicken breasts, skinned and cut into chunks

2 onions, finely chopped

3 garlic cloves, chopped

2 tsp ground cumin

½ tsp cayenne pepper

1 tsp each of: ground ginger, ground coriander and curcuma (turmeric)

²/3 cup / 100 g ground almonds

2 cups / 500 ml chicken broth (stock)

Salt and pepper

½ cup / 125 ml yogurt

1 cup / 75 g flaked almonds

1 tsp saffron threads, to garnish

2 tbsp sesame seeds, lightly toasted in a dry pan, to garnish

Method

Prep and cook time: 45 min

1. Heat the oil in a wide pan and fry the chicken pieces for 5 minutes or until lightly browned all over. Remove from the pan and keep warm.

2. Gently fry the onions in the pan until softened but not brown then stir in the garlic and spices. Cook for 2 minutes, stirring all the time.

3. Add the ground almonds and chicken broth (stock), season with salt and pepper then add the chicken and simmer very gently for 20 minutes.

4. Spoon in the yogurt and flaked almonds and simmer very gently for 5 more minutes.

5. Serve the soup in warmed bowls with the saffron threads and sesame seeds sprinkled over.

PUMPKIN SOUP WITH CHICKEN

Ingredients

2 chicken breasts, sliced into thin strips

1–2 tbsp light soy sauce

1 onion, sliced

¾ inch / 2 cm piece of fresh ginger, finely chopped

1 small pumpkin, diced

2 cups / 500 ml vegetable broth (stock)

1 red chili, sliced in half lengthwise

1¾ cups / 400 ml coconut milk

Salt & freshly milled pepper

2–3 tomatoes, de-seeded and choppped

Thai basil, to garnish

Method

Prep and cook time: 45 min

1. Marinate the chicken in 1–2 tablespoons of soy sauce while you prepare the vegetables.

2. Put the onion, ginger, pumpkin and chili into a pan with the vegetable broth (stock). Cook for about 20 minutes with a lid on the pan. Then remove the chili and take half of the vegetables out of the broth (stock).

3. Finely purée the rest of the vegetables with the broth (stock). Pour in the coconut milk. Bring to a boil. Boil for 2–3 minutes, then return the vegetables to the soup.

4. Add the tomatoes to the soup with the sliced chicken. Briefly bring to a boil, then cook gently for about 7 minutes or until the chicken is cooked.

5. Season to taste and ladle into bowls. Serve garnished with basil.

CHICKEN AND MUSHROOM SOUP WITH WATERCRESS

Ingredients

2 tbsp olive oil

7 oz / 200 g chicken breast, skinned and finely diced

1 onion, chopped

1 garlic clove, chopped

2 celery sticks, chopped

10 oz / 300 g button mushrooms, roughly chopped, reserve some for garnish

1 tbsp chopped fresh thyme

1 tbsp dry sherry

3 cups / 700 ml chicken broth (stock)

2 tbsp cream

watercress, to garnish

Method

Prep and cook time: 25 min

1. Heat the oil in a large pan and fry the chicken for 5 minutes or until golden brown all over. Remove from the pan and set aside.

2. Add the onion, garlic and celery to the pan and cook for 5 minutes.

3. Add the chopped mushrooms, thyme and sherry. Season to taste and cook the vegetables for 2-3 minutes, stirring occasionally.

4. Transfer the mixture to a food processor or blender and add half the broth (stock). Process until smooth, then return to the pan and add the remaining broth. Return the chicken to the pan and heat until boiling. Simmer for 3 minutes. Stir in the cream and heat through.

5. Ladle into bowls or mugs and top with the reserved mushrooms and the watercress

SWEET POTATO AND SQUASH SOUP WITH CHICKEN

Ingredients

2 tomatoes

2 tsp olive oil

1 small onion, chopped

3½ cups / 800 ml vegetable broth (stock) or water

12 oz / 300 g butternut squash, peeled, deseeded, and chopped

1 medium sweet potato, peeled and roughly chopped

1 skinless, boneless chicken breast, chopped

Method

Prep and cook time: 40 min

1. Bring a medium saucepan of water to a boil; drop in the tomatoes and heat for 1–3 minutes until the tomato skins split. Remove the tomatoes with a slotted spoon; when cool enough to handle, peel and coarsely chop.

2. Heat the oil in a large saucepan or soup pot; add the onion and fry for a few minutes to soften (do not brown).

3. Add the broth (stock) or water, squash, sweet potato, tomatoes and chicken. Cover and simmer for 15 minutes until the vegetables are soft.

4. Remove a ladleful of the vegetables and reserve. Use a stick (immersion) blender to whiz the rest of the soup to a smooth purée (or transfer in batches to a blender or food processor). Return the reserved vegetables to the soup and serve.

CHICKEN SOUP WITH BEAN SPROUTS

Ingredients

For the curry paste:

1 chili

1 shallot

½ tsp chopped lemongrass

1 tsp freshly grated ginger

Good pinch cumin

1 tsp ground curcuma (turmeric)

For the soup:

14 oz / 400 g chicken breast fillet

2 garlic cloves

¾ inch / 2 cm piece of fresh ginger

1 stalk lemongrass

2 tbsp oil

¼ cups / 200 g soybean sprouts

1¾ cups / 400 ml chicken broth (stock)

1¾ cups / 400 ml unsweetened coconut milk

2 tbsp fish sauce

2 tbsp lime juice

Fresh mint leaves, to garnish

Method

Prep and cook time: 20 min

1. Put all the curry paste ingredients into a mortar and grind to a paste.

2. Poach the chicken in simmering salted water for 5–8 minutes. Take out of the water and let drain. Tear the meat into pieces in the direction of the grain.

3. Peel and finely chop the garlic and ginger. Crush the lemongrass. Heat the oil in a wok. Put the meat, ginger, garlic and lemongrass into the wok and fry briefly.

4. Add the bean sprouts and fry briefly then stir in the chicken broth (stock). Add the coconut milk and 1 tablespoon of the curry paste and bring to a boil.

5. Draw the wok away from the heat and season with lime juice and fish sauce. Remove the lemongrass.

6. Ladle the soup into bowls and serve garnished with mint leaves.

CHICKEN AND VEGETABLE WRAPS

Ingredients

For the sauce:

6 tbsp tomato ketchup

2 tbsp tomato relish or red bell pepper relish

Salt & freshly milled pepper

1 tsp chopped dried mixed herbs

1 clove garlic, crushed

For the tortillas:

2 small chicken breasts

Salt & freshly milled pepper

3 tbsp oil

2 carrots, cut into sticks

1 bunch scallions (spring onions), cut in half lengthways

1 red bell pepper, cut into strips

12 tortillas, about 6 inches / 15 cm in diameter

Method

Prep and cook time: 30 min

1. Place all ingredients for the sauce in a bowl and mix. Set aside.

2. Season the chicken breasts with salt and pepper and fry in oil for 7–10 minutes, until cooked. Take out of the skillet and sauté the vegetables in the oil. Season with salt and pepper. Cut the meat into thin strips and mix with the vegetables. Keep warm over a low heat.

3. In the meantime, place the tortillas in the microwave or in a dry skillet and heat.

4. Place the tortillas next to each other on the work surface. Spoon some of the chicken and vegetable mixture down the center of each tortilla and drizzle a little sauce over the top. Fold the bottom end over, and then roll each tortilla up tightly. Place in glasses and serve.

CHICKEN PASTIES

Ingredients

For the pastry:

¼ cup / 50 g butter, chopped

2½ cups / 250 g all-purpose (plain) flour

3 tbsp olive oil

½ tsp salt

For the filling:

3 tbsp oil

1 onion, finely chopped

9 oz / 250 g ground (minced) chicken

1½ cups / 150 g feta cheese, crumbled

1 tbsp pine nuts, chopped

2 egg yolks

Oil, for brushing

Salt and freshly ground pepper

Method

Prep and cook time: 50 min

1. Rub the butter into the flour until the mixture resembles breadcrumbs. Add the oil, salt and enough water to make a dough. Wrap in plastic wrap (clingfilm) and chill for 20 minutes.

2. Meanwhile, make the filling. Heat the oil in a pan and gently cook the onion until translucent. Add the chicken and cook, stirring, until the meat is well browned.

3. Remove from the heat and stir in the feta cheese, pine nuts and egg yolks. Season with salt and pepper and set aside.

4. Heat the oven to 375F (180C / Gas Mark 5).

5. Roll out the pastry thinly and cut circles about 10 cm/4 inches in diameter with a cutter. Place a little filling on each circle, moisten the edge with a little water, fold over to form semi-circles and press the join closed with a fork.

6. Place the pasties on a greased cookie sheet, brush with a little oil and bake for 15–20 minutes or until golden brown.

Makes 20

CHICKEN AND VEGETABLE QUESADILLAS

Ingredients

1 red bell pepper, diced

1 cup / 150 g black beans, canned, drained

2 chicken breasts, chopped

2 scallions (spring onions), trimmed and cut into rings

4 large tortillas

1²/₃ cups / 200 g grated cheese, such as Cheddar

Salt & pepper

Method

Prep and cook time: 45 min

1. Preheat the oven to 320°F (160°C / Gas Mark 3).

2. Mix the bell pepper, beans, chicken and scallions (spring onions).

3. Lay two tortillas on a cookie sheet lined with baking parchment and scatter with half of the cheese. Divide the mixed chicken and vegetables between the two tortillas, season with salt and pepper and finish off with the rest of the cheese. Put another tortilla on top of each and press lightly. Bake in the oven for 20–25 minutes. Halve the quesadillas and serve.

CHICKEN SALAD PITAS

Ingredients

1 small grilled or roasted chicken

Scant 1 cup / 200 g mayonnaise

Scant ½ cup / 100 g sour cream

½ bunch parsley (about 1 oz / 25 g), chopped (reserve a few whole leaves for garnish)

1 red onion, coarsely chopped

1 tart green apple, cored, cut into eighths, and thinly sliced

1 garlic clove, minced

Salt and freshly ground pepper

4 pita breads, halved and split to make pockets

4–6 lettuce leaves

Method
Prep and cook time: 30 min

1. Skin the chicken, take the meat off the bone and shred or cut the meat into small pieces.

2. Combine in a bowl with the mayonnaise, sour cream, parsley, onion, apple and garlic; season with salt and pepper. Line the pita pockets with lettuce leaves, then stuff with the salad. Serve at once, garnished with parsley leaves.

CHICKEN AND MUSHROOMS ON TOASTED CIABATTA

Ingredients

2 tbsp olive oil

2 chicken breasts, skinned and diced

1 red bell pepper, deseeded and sliced

8 oz / 200 g canned button mushrooms, sliced

$2/3$ cup / 100 g frozen peas, thawed

1 onion, sliced

1 cup / 100 g grated cheese

1 pinch curry powder

2 ciabattas, split horizontally

Method
Prep and cook time: 30 min

1. Heat the oven to 400°F (200°C / Gas Mark 6).

2. Heat the oil in a pan and quickly fry the chicken until lightly browned.

3. Stir in the bell pepper, mushrooms, peas, onion, cheese and curry powder, season with salt and pepper and pile the mixture onto the sliced ciabattas.

4. Bake in the oven for 10–15 minutes, or until the chicken is cooked through.

CHICKEN NACHOS WITH DIPS

Ingredients

For the guacamole:

2 avocados, peeled and stones removed

1 small onion, very finely chopped

1 green chili pepper, deseeded and finely chopped

2 tbsp yogurt

1 tbsp finely chopped cilantro (coriander)

Juice of 2 limes

For the nachos:

2 tbsp vegetable oil

1 clove garlic, finely chopped

1 tsp paprika

2 chicken breasts, skinned and cut into chunks

¼ iceberg lettuce, shredded

4 tomatoes, seeds removed and roughly chopped

8 nacho shells

1 cup / 100 g grated cheese, to serve

4 tomatoes, roughly chopped, to serve

Method

Prep and cook time: 45 min

1. For the guacamole, mash the avocados and beat in the rest of the ingredients. Season with salt and pepper and set aside.

2. For the nachos, heat the oil in a skillet and gently fry the garlic and paprika for 1 minute. Add the chicken pieces and cook, stirring all the time, for 4–5 minutes or until the chicken is cooked through. Season with salt and pepper.

3. Stir the tomatoes into the chicken and fill the nachos with the mixture along with a little shredded lettuce.

4. Serve the nachos with the guacamole, grated cheese and chopped tomatoes alongside.

SPRING ROLLS WITH CHILI DIP

Ingredients

For the filling:

4 oz / 100 g glass noodles

8 oz / 250 g carrots, grated

8 oz / 250 g white cabbage, finely shredded

1¼ cups / 200 g soy bean sprouts

3 garlic cloves, chopped

4 cups / 1 liter oil, to fry

7 oz / 200 g ground (minced) chicken

Salt & freshly milled pepper

2 tsp sugar

1 egg

About 40 spring roll wrappers

For the dip:

1 jar Thai sweet chili dip

Method

Prep and cook time: 50 min

1. Soak the glass noodles in cold water for 30 minutes. Put the carrots, cabbage and bean sprouts into a bow and mix.

2. Heat 3 tablespoons of the oil in a skillet or wok and briefly fry the garlic. Add the ground chicken and fry for 3–5 minutes, breaking it up until brown all over. Season with salt and pepper and leave to cool slightly.

3. Drain the glass noodles, cut into about 2 inch (4 cm) lengths and add to the vegetables. Season with salt, pepper and a little sugar. Add the cooled ground meat and mix well.

4. Lightly beat the egg. Take 1 spring roll wrapper and place on a work surface. Put about 2 heaped tablespoons of the filling across the middle of the wrapper. Turn in the sides and roll up to make a roll about 4 inches (10 cm) long. Use a little beaten egg to stick the edge of the spring roll. Repeat with the other wrappers.

5. Heat the remaining oil in a wok or skillet. (The oil is hot enough when bubbles form on the handle of a wooden spoon held in the oil.) Fry the spring rolls in batches for about 6–8 minutes until golden brown. Take out, drain on a paper towel and serve with chili dip.

CHICKEN IN TEMPURA BATTER

Ingredients

1 cup / 100 g all purpose (plain) flour

1 tsp baking powder

1 egg white, lightly beaten

1 scallion (spring onion), very finely chopped

Approx 1 cup / 250 ml sparkling mineral water, chilled

2 cups / 500 ml vegetable oil

½ red bell pepper, deseeded and finely diced

½ green bell pepper, deseeded and finely diced

½ yellow bell pepper, deseeded and finely diced

4 chicken breasts, skinned and cut into chunks

3 tbsp cornstarch (cornflour)

Soy sauce for dipping

Method

Prep and cook time: 30 min

1. Beat the flour with the baking powder, egg white, scallion (spring onion) and enough sparkling water to make a batter. Set aside.

2. Heat about 3 tbsp of the oil in a wok or large skillet and cook the diced bell peppers for 2 minutes. Remove from the pan, drain on kitchen paper and keep warm.

3. Toss the chicken chunks in the cornstarch (cornflour), shaking off any excess.

4. Add the rest of the oil to the wok and heat until smoking.

5. Dip the chicken chunks into the batter and fry in batches until golden brown and the chicken is cooked through.

6. Drain on kitchen paper and serve with the bell peppers scattered over and the soy sauce for dipping.

CHICKEN AND PUMPKIN PATTIES

Ingredients

1 lb / 450 g pumpkin

6 shallots

4 tbsp olive oil

3 tsp garam masala

1 lb / 450 g ground (minced) chicken

3 cups / 150 g wholemeal breadcrumbs

1 cup / 25 g chopped fresh parsley

2 eggs

3–4 tbsp all-purpose (plain) flour

Salt and pepper

Method

Prep and cook time: 40 min

1. Peel the pumpkin and discard the seeds. Coarsely grate the flesh and put in a large bowl. Finely chop the shallots.

2. Heat 1 tbsp of the oil in a skillet (frying pan) and gently fry the shallots until translucent.

3. Add the garam masala and cook for 2 minutes, then remove from the heat and leave to cool.

4. Add the chicken, breadcrumbs, parsley, eggs, 2 tbsp of the flour and the cooled shallots to the pumpkin and mix together. Season with salt and pepper.

5. Put the remaining flour on to a large plate. Form the chicken mixture into 16–20 patties and lightly coat each one in the flour.

6. Heat the remaining oil in a skillet and fry the patties for 4 minutes on each side, ensuring the chicken is cooked through.

CHICKEN AND CORN FRITTERS

Ingredients

14 oz / 400 g can corn kernels

5¼ oz / 150 g ground (minced) chicken

2 cloves garlic, peeled

1 tbsp sugar

About 1 tbsp cornstarch (cornflour)

2 eggs

Fish sauce

Cayenne pepper

Oil for deep-frying

Toothpicks (cocktail sticks)

Method
Prep and cook time: 20 min

1. Drain the corn kernels well. Finely purée half of the corn with the ground (minced) chicken, garlic, sugar, eggs and 1 tablespoon cornstarch (cornflour).

2. Then mix in the rest of the corn kernels and add a little more cornstarch if needed (fry a small test fritter if necessary).

3. Season with fish sauce and cayenne pepper. Heat the oil and fry for 2–3 minutes, turning occasionally, until golden brown.

4. Drain on paper towel and serve speared on toothpicks (cocktail sticks).

CHICKEN KEBABS WITH PEANUT SAUCE

Ingredients

½ cup / 125 ml sesame oil

1 garlic clove, chopped

2 red chilis, chopped

2 tbsp honey

1 cup / 250 ml smooth peanut butter

1 tbsp soy sauce

1 tsp fish sauce

Juice of 2 limes

2 chicken breasts, skinned and sliced

1 tbsp light oil

Chilis and lime wedges, to garnish

Method
Prep and cook time: 25 min

1. Heat the oil in a small pan and gently cook the garlic and chilis until soft. Stir in the honey, peanut butter, soy sauce, fish sauce and lime juice. Bring to a boil and simmer for 5 minutes.

2. Thread the chicken strips onto wooden skewers and brush with a little oil.

3. Heat a griddle pan and cook the chicken skewers until browned and cooked through.

4. Serve the chicken skewers drizzled with the sauce, garnish with whole chilis and lime wedges, and serve the remaining sauce alongside for dipping.

CHICKEN WITH BELL PEPPER SAUCE

Ingredients

½ cup / 125 ml oil

Juice of 2 limes

2 tbsp honey

1 red chili, seeds removed and chopped

2 chicken breasts, skinned

2 orange bell peppers

1 garlic clove

Salt and freshly ground pepper

Lime zest, to garnish

Method

Prep and cook time: 45 min

1. Whisk together 6 tbsp of oil with the lime juice, honey and chopped chili to make a marinade.

2. Cut the chicken into bite-size pieces, mix with the marinade and set aside.

3. Brush the bell peppers with a little oil and place under a hot broiler (grill) until the skins are charred all over, turning frequently. Put in a bowl, cover with plastic wrap (clingfilm) and set aside.

4. Heat 2 tbsp of oil in a pan and gently fry the garlic for 2 minutes.

5. Remove and discard the pepper skins and seeds. Place the peppers in a food processor with the garlic and blend well. Season with salt and pepper and set aside.

6. Remove the chicken from the marinade. Heat the remaining oil in a skillet and fry the chicken pieces for about 6 minutes or until browned on all sides and cooked through.

7. Mix the peppers and garlic with the reserved marinade, heat quickly in the skillet and drizzle over the chicken pieces. Scatter with lime zest and serve immediately.

HONEY AND MUSTARD CHICKEN WINGS WITH SESAME SEEDS

Ingredients

3 tbsp olive oil

4 tbsp honey

2 tbsp Dijon mustard

Juice of 1 lemon

12 chicken wings

4 tbsp sesame seeds

Salt and freshly ground pepper

Method

Prep and cook time: 30 min plus
1 hour to marinate

1. Whisk together the oil, honey, mustard and lemon juice to make a marinade. Season with salt and pepper.

2. Put the chicken wings into a large bowl, pour over the marinade and mix well. Set aside for at least 1 hour, turning from time to time.

3. Heat the oven to 400F (200C / Gas Mark 6).

4. Toast the sesame seeds in a dry skillet until lightly browned. Set aside.

5. Remove the chicken wings from the marinade and put onto a cookie sheet. Roast in the oven for 15–20 minutes, turning once, until cooked through and browned all over.

6. Sprinkle the chicken wings with the toasted sesame seeds and serve warm or cold.

PAPRIKA CHICKEN WITH ONIONS

Ingredients

6 tbsp olive oil

1 onion, finely diced

1 garlic clove, chopped

1 tsp paprika

2 chicken breasts, skinned and cut into bite-size pieces

1 tbsp balsamic vinegar

Cilantro (fresh coriander) sprigs, to garnish

Method

Prep and cook time: 20 min

1. Heat the oil in a pan and gently fry the onion until translucent. Add the garlic and paprika and cook for 1 more minute.

2. Turn up the heat, add the chicken pieces and cook for about 6 minutes, stirring frequently, until the chicken is browned and cooked through.

3. Add the balsamic vinegar, stir and cook for a further 2–3 minutes. Serve immediately, with cilantro (fresh coriander) to garnish.

GRILLED CHICKEN WITH MANGO DIP

Ingredients

16 chicken wings

For the marinade:

Few dashes Tabasco sauce

4 tbsp oil

1 tbsp honey

1 tbsp ketchup

2 tbsp chili sauce

1 tbsp vinegar

Salt & freshly milled pepper

1 scallion (spring onion), finely chopped

For the mango dip:

1 mango

1 tbsp honey

1 tbsp rosemary leaves

Lime juice, to taste

Method

Prep and cook time: 45 min plus 8 hours to marinate

1. For the marinade, mix the Tabasco sauce, oil, honey, ketchup, chili sauce and vinegar. Season well with salt and pepper and stir in the scallions (spring onions).

2. Brush the chicken with the marinade. Cover and marinate, preferably overnight. Then cook on a grill over a medium heat for 15–20 minutes, turning frequently.

3. For the mango dip, finely purée the flesh of a mango with 1 tablespoon honey and 1 tablespoon of rosemary leaves. Add a little lime juice to taste.

4. Serve the chicken wings with a separate dish of mango dip.

CHICKEN NUGGETS

Ingredients

1 lb 6 oz / 600 g chicken breast, cut into bite-size pieces

Salt & freshly milled pepper

3–4 tbsp all-purpose (plain) flour

2 eggs

2 cups breadcrumbs, to coat

Fat for frying

Chili sauce or tomato ketchup, to serve

Method
Prep and cook time: 30 min

1. Season the chicken with salt and pepper then lightly coat them with flour.

2. Whisk the eggs in a bowl. Place the breadcrumbs on a plate. Coat the chicken pieces with egg, then roll in the breadcrumbs and press down well.

3. Fry the nuggets in hot fat for 3–4 minutes until the chicken is cooked. Drain on a paper towel. Serve with chili sauce or tomato ketchup.

CHICK PEA SALAD WITH SATAY CHICKEN

Ingredients

3 tbsp smooth peanut butter

½ cup / 125 ml olive oil

1 tbsp honey

Juice of 1 lime

2 chicken breasts, skinned and cut into strips

4 cups / 800 g canned chickpeas, drained and rinsed

2 red onions, finely chopped

2 red chilies, seeds removed and finely chopped

1 cup / 25 g chopped parsley

Juice of 1 lemon

Salt and freshly ground pepper

Method

Prep and cook time: 15 min plus 30 min to marinate

1. Blend the peanut butter with 2 tbsp of oil, the honey and the lime juice. Pour over the chicken strips, mix well and set aside for 30 minutes.

2. Mix the chickpeas with the chopped onion, chilis and parsley. Mix the remaining oil with the lemon juice, season with salt and pepper and pour over the chickpeas.

3. Remove the chicken strips from the marinade and thread onto wooden skewers.

4. Cook the chicken under a hot broiler (grill) for 5 minutes or until cooked through, turning once. Serve with the chickpea salad.

SALADS

GREEK SALAD WITH GRILLED CHICKEN

Ingredients

For the chicken:

4 chicken breasts, skinned and sliced in half horizontally

2 tbsp vegetable oil

2 tbsp honey

1 tbsp lemon juice

½ tsp paprika

Salt and pepper

For the salad:

5 tbsp olive oil

2 tbsp lemon juice

1 tsp dried oregano

1 red onion, cut into wedges

½ cucumber, sliced

4 tomatoes, cut into wedges

1 cup / 100 g black olives

1 handful baby spinach

8 oz / 225 g feta cheese, crumbled

1 red bell pepper, deseeded and sliced

½ cup / 50 g pine nuts, lightly toasted

Method

Prep and cook time: 15 min plus
30 min marinading time

1. Mix together the vegetable oil, honey, lemon juice and paprika with a little salt and pepper. Mix in the chicken thoroughly, ensuring the pieces are coated with the marinade and set aside for 30 minutes.

2. For the salad, mix together the olive oil, lemon juice and dried oregano to make a dressing. Season with salt and pepper and set aside. Mix together the remaining salad ingredients in a large bowl.

3. Heat the broiler or a griddle pan and cook the chicken for about 3 minutes each side, turning once to make a crisscross pattern, or until the chicken is cooked through.

4. Drizzle the dressing over the salad, mix in the chicken and serve.

GRILLED CHICKEN WITH MANGO SALSA

Ingredients

1 pear, peeled, cored and diced

1 mango, peeled, stoned removed and diced

1 red bell pepper, deseeded and diced

1 red chili, deseeded and finely chopped

Juice of 2 limes

4 sprigs parsley, chopped

3 tbsp vegetable oil

2 chicken breast fillets

Lime wedges, to garnish

Method

Prep and cook time: 30 min

1. Mix together the diced pear, mango, bell pepper, chili and lime juice. Season with salt and pepper, stir in the chopped parsley and set aside.

2. Heat the oil in a griddle pan or wide skillet and cook the chicken for about 4 minutes on each side or until the chicken is cooked through.

3. Slice the chicken breasts and serve with the mango salsa and garnish with lime wedges.

CHICKEN AND RED CABBAGE SALAD

Ingredients

½ cup / 100 g wild rice

2 tbsp balsamic vinegar

1 tbsp raspberry vinegar

1 tbsp honey

Juice of half a lemon

½ red cabbage, trimmed, core removed and finely shredded

¾ cup / 150 g dates, roughly chopped

4 tbsp sunflower oil

2 chicken breasts, skin on

2 zucchini (courgettes), cut into chunks

2 tbsp sesame seeds

Method

Prep and cook time: 40 min

1. Cook the wild rice according to the packet instructions, drain well and set aside.

2. Mix the vinegars, honey and lemon juice together, season with salt and pepper and stir into the red cabbage. Add the dates and cooked rice and set aside.

3. Heat 2 tbsp of oil in a wide skillet and cook the chicken breasts gently for about 4 minutes each side or until cooked through. Remove and discard the skin, cut the meat into chunks and add to the cabbage mixture.

4. Heat the remaining oil in the skillet and gently cook the zucchini (courgettes) until softened. Stir into the cabbage, check the seasoning and place in serving bowls.

5. Scatter over the sesame seeds and serve.

GRILLED CHICKEN WITH TABBOULEH

Ingredients

For the chicken:

2 chicken breasts

Juice of 1 lemon

1 tsp honey

2 tsp grain mustard

For the tabbouleh:

1 cup / 150 g couscous

1¹/₃ cups / 300 ml chicken broth (stock)

6 tbsp olive oil

1 red onion, finely chopped

1 garlic clove, finely chopped

1 bunch mint

½ bunch flat-leaf parsley

1 cucumber, peeled and diced

Juice of 1 lemon

Method

Prep and cook time: 35 min

1. Put the chicken breasts between two sheets of plastic wrap (clingfilm) and bash with a rolling pan to flatten.

2. Mix together the lemon juice, honey and mustard, rub into the chicken breasts and leave to marinade for 15 minutes.

3. Place the couscous into a bowl, add the boiling broth (stock) and leave to soak for 10 minutes.

4. Heat 1 tbsp of oil and fry the onion until translucent then add the garlic and cook for 2 minutes. Let cool slightly and add to the couscous.

5. Add the herbs and cucumber to the couscous and drizzle with oil and lemon juice. Mix well and season to taste with salt and pepper.

6. Heat a griddle pan until very hot then cook the chicken for about 3 minutes each side, or until cooked through, turning once to make a crisscross pattern.

7. Slice the chicken and serve with the tabbouleh.

PAPAYA SALAD WITH CHICKEN AND SHRIMP

Ingredients

1 papaya, preferably green

14 oz / 400 g snake beans / long beans, trimmed

2 tbsp sesame oil

4 oz / 100 g peeled shrimps (prawns), ready to cook

1 red bell pepper, cut into strips

1½ cups / 240 g soybean sprouts

4 oz / 100 g cooked chicken, shredded

²/3 cup / 100 g unsalted peanuts, roughly chopped

Cayenne pepper

Light soy sauce

Method

Prep and cook time: 20 min

1. Peel the papaya, discarding the seeds and grate finely.

2. Blanch the beans in boiling, salted for about 8 minutes, until al dente.

3. Heat the oil in a skillet and gently fry the shrimps (prawns) for 1–2 minutes. Add the bell pepper, soybean sprouts and beans and sweat briefly. Add the cooked chicken, papaya and the chopped peanuts and season to taste with soy sauce and cayenne pepper.

4. Serve in pre-warmed bowls.

GLASS NOODLES WITH CHICKEN AND MINT

Ingredients

2 cups / 200 g glass noodles

3–4 kaffir lime leaves

12 oz / 350 g chicken breast fillet

2 scallions (spring onions)

2 tbsp / 30 ml sesame oil

2 inches / 5 cm ginger, finely chopped

1–2 cloves garlic, finely chopped

3–4 shallots, finely chopped

2 red chilis, deseeded fnd finely chopped (wear gloves)

2 tbsp brown sugar

Juice of 2 limes

1 small cucumber, peeled and thinly sliced

2 handfuls herbs (mint, cilantro (coriander), Thai basil)

2 limes, halved

$1/3$ cup / 50 g unsalted peanuts, roasted

Salt & pepper

Method

Prep and cook time: 40 min

1. Soak the glass noodles in lukewarm water and cut into smaller lengths with scissors. In a small pan heat about 4 cups (1 liter) water with the kaffir lime leaves and 1 teaspoon salt. Add the chicken breast and simmer gently over a low heat until cooked (12–15 minutes). Drain, let the meat cool slightly, then tear into small pieces.

2. Drain the glass noodles and cook in salted water, then refresh in cold water and drain well. Peel and shred the scallions (spring onions). Soak in cold water.

3. Heat the oil in a skillet and sauté the ginger, garlic, shallots and chilis for 2–3 minutes. Stir in the sugar, sauté briefly, then add the glass noodles, chicken and lime juice. Season with pepper, mix well and set aside.

4. Drain the scallions and mix them into the chicken and noodles along with the cucumber and herbs. Pile the salad on plates and serve garnished with lime halves and scattered with peanuts.

SWEET AND SOUR CHICKEN SALAD

Ingredients

For the dressing:

2 tbsp honey

4 tbsp olive oil

Finely grated zest and juice of
1 orange

2 tbsp sweet chili sauce

Salt and freshly ground pepper

For the salad:

4 cooked smoked chicken breasts, cut
into chunks

2 cups / 400 g drained canned or
thawed frozen corn kernels

1 cucumber, cut into bite-size chunks

1 clementine / mandarin orange,
peeled and segmented

1 large carrot, sliced into matchsticks

5 oz / 150 g mixed salad greens

Deep fried rice noodles (rice sticks),
to garnish

Method
Prep and cook time: 20 min

1. To make the dressing spoon the honey into a small jar with a tightly fitting lid. Add the oil, orange zest and juice and sweet chili sauce. Season with salt and ground black pepper and shake to mix.

2. Place the chicken, corn, cucumber, clementine (mandarin orange), carrots and salad leaves into large bowl. Toss together.

3. Drizzle with the dressing and garnish with the rice noodles.

CHICKEN WITH LIME AND MINT

Ingredients

6 tbsp lime juice

1 tbsp fish sauce

2 tsp sugar

4 boneless chicken breasts, skinned

1 carrot, cut into ribbons

1 small zucchini (courgette), cut into ribbons

1 cup / 20 g fresh mint leaves

3 tbsp olive oil

1 red chili, deseeded and finely chopped

Lime zest, to garnish

Method

Prep and cook time: 30 min
plus 30 min to marinate

1. Put 3 tbsp of the lime juice, the fish sauce and sugar in a bowl and mix together. Rub into the chicken breasts. Leave to marinate for about 30 minutes, turning from time to time.

2. Put the carrot ribbons, zucchini ribbons and mint leaves in a large bowl. Mix 1 tbsp oil with the remaining lime juice. Add to the bowl and toss together. Put into serving bowls.

4. Heat the remaining oil in a skillet (frying pan). Remove the chicken from the marinade, add to the pan and fry for about 5 minutes on each side until tender and cooked through.

5. Thickly slice the chicken breasts widthways and arrange on top of the vegetables. Sprinkle with the chopped chili and serve garnished with lime zest. If desired, serve warm with rice noodles.

SMOKED CHICKEN AND MANGO SALAD

Ingredients

1 cucumber

2 scallions (spring onions)

3–4 oz / 100 g bean sprouts

Salt and pepper

1 mango

4 cooked smoked boneless chicken breasts

6 tbsp shop-bought French dressing

3 tbsp sweet chili sauce

4 little gem lettuces

Method

Prep and cook time: 20 min

1. Cut the cucumber in half lengthways and then into slices. Shred the scallions (spring onions). Put the cucumber and scallions into a large bowl and add the bean sprouts. Season with salt and pepper.

2. Peel and slice the mango flesh either side of the stone, and then cut into thin slices.

3 Shred the chicken. Add the chicken and mango to the salad ingredients and mix together.

4. Pour the French dressing into a screw-top jar, add the sweet chili sauce and shake together. Toss the salad in the dressing.

5. Arrange the little lettuce leaves in the base of a large salad bowl. Spoon the salad on top and serve.

CHICKEN, AVOCADO AND STRAWBERRY SALAD

Ingredients

For the dressing:

3 tbsp white wine vinegar

1 tbsp lemon juice

3 tbsp sunflower oil

1 tbsp rapeseed oil

Salt and pepper

Half an iceberg lettuce

8 oz / 225 g strawberries

1 cup / 100 g seedless grapes

1 avocado

4 boneless chicken breasts, skinned

½ tbsp / 10 g butter

1 tsp curry powder

1 tsp dried thyme

Salt and pepper

Method

Prep and cook time: 30 min

1. To make the dressing, put the vinegar, lemon juice, sunflower and rapeseed oil in a large bowl and mix together. Season with salt and pepper.

2. Tear the lettuce leaves into bite-size pieces and arrange on serving plates. Hull and slice the strawberries. Halve the grapes. Cut the avocado in half lengthways and slice the flesh.

3. Add the avocado and strawberries to the dressing and carefully mix together. Add the grapes.

4. Slice the chicken into strips. Heat the butter in a skillet (frying pan) and gently fry the chicken slices for about 5 minutes until lightly browned on all sides.

5. Add the curry powder and thyme and season with salt and pepper. Cook gently for a further 4–5 minutes until the chicken is tender and cooked through.

6. Arrange the meat on top of the lettuce. Pour the dressed avocado and strawberries on top and serve at once.

CHICKEN CAESAR SALAD

Ingredients

4 garlic cloves

2 egg yolks

2 anchovy fillets

2 tbsp lemon juice

Salt and pepper

8 tbsp olive oil

2 tbsp chopped fresh parsley

½ cup / 50 g grated
Parmesan cheese

2 boneless chicken breasts, skinned

2 tbsp vegetable oil

3 slices day-old white bread

1 stick / 120 g butter

1 romaine (cos) lettuce

Method

Prep and cook time: 45 min

1. For the dressing, crush 3 garlic cloves and put in a bowl with the egg yolks.

2. Rinse the anchovies in cool water and chop finely. Add to the egg yolks with the lemon juice, salt and pepper. Beat until creamy.

3. Sir in the oil, drop by drop, until the dressing thickens.

4. Add the parsley and cheese and mix together. Set aside.

5. Season the chicken with salt and pepper. Heat the oil in a skillet (frying pan) and fry the chicken for about 5 minutes on each side or until cooked through. Remove the chicken from the skillet and set aside.

6. Cut the bread into small cubes. Wipe the skillet with paper towels and rub the remaining garlic clove over base. Add the butter and fry the bread cubes until crunchy. Remove the cubes from the pan.

7. Tear the lettuce leaves into bite-size pieces and toss together with the dressing. Cut the chicken diagonally into slices and serve alongside the salad. Sprinkle the bread croûtons on top to garnish.

SPINACH AND CHICKEN SALAD

Ingredients

2 boneless chicken breasts, skinned

2 tbsp light soy sauce

2 nori seaweed leaves

4 oz / 120 g cooked ham

1 red bell pepper

1 lb / 450 g fresh baby spinach

4 tbsp sesame oil

2 tbsp rice wine vinegar

Salt and pepper

2 tbsp sunflower oil

2 tbsp sesame seeds

Method

Prep and cook time: 35 min plus
20 min to marinate

1. Cut the chicken breasts into bite-size pieces and put in a bowl. Add the soy sauce and leave to marinate for 20 minutes.

2. Meanwhile, slice the nori leaves and ham into thin strips. Finely slice the red pepper, discarding the core and seeds. Rinse the spinach and shake to remove excess water.

3. To make the dressing, put the sesame oil rice wine vinegar, salt and pepper in a jug and whisk together.

4. Heat the sunflower oil in a skillet (frying pan), add the chicken pieces and fry until golden brown all over and cooked through.

5. Mix the spinach with the red pepper and toss in the dressing. Add more seasoning if wished. Carefully toss the chicken with the spinach.

6. Arrange the salad on serving plates. Garnish with the ham and nori strips and sprinkle the sesame seeds on top. Serve at once.

CHICKEN SALAD WITH BEET LEAVES

Ingredients

4 chicken breasts, cut into strips

4 tbsp olive oil, plus oil for frying

2 tbsp cider vinegar

1 tbsp coarse Dijon mustard

Salt & freshly milled pepper

2 cups / 200 g lamb's lettuce

2 cups / 200 g beet (beetroot) leaves

1 yellow bell pepper, deseeded
and chopped into cubes

2 beefsteak tomatoes, cut
into wedges

Method
Prep and cook time: 25 min

1. Heat a little olive oil in a skillet and fry
the chicken for about 1–2 minutes on all
sides until cooked thoroughly. Season with
salt and pepper and place on the side.

2. Make a vinaigrette dressing using
the 4 tbsp olive oil, cider vinegar, Dijon
mustard, and salt and pepper. Place the
lamb's lettuce, beetroot leaves, bell pepper,
tomatoes and chicken in a bowl, pour in the
vinaigrette dressing and toss. Season to taste
with salt and pepper and serve.

THAI CHICKEN SALAD

Ingredients

2 green chilies, seeded and chopped (wear gloves to prevent irritation)

1 shallot, thinly sliced

1 tsp shrimp paste

½ tsp freshly grated ginger root

1 lb / 450 g chicken legs or thighs, skinned, boned, and sliced into strips

8 cups / 400 g mixed salad greens

1 handful cilantro (coriander) leaves

1 handful mint leaves

1 bunch scallions (spring onions), chopped

1 tsp finely grated lemongrass, plus additional slivers to garnish

2 tbsp vegetable oil

1 onion, chopped

2 tomatoes, sliced into wedges

2 tbsp fish sauce

2 tbsp lime juice

1 tbsp brown sugar

Method

Prep and cook time: 20 min

1. Prepare the Thai curry paste: grind the chilies, shallot, shrimp paste and ginger to a paste with a mortar and pestle or in a spice grinder. Transfer to a bowl and add the chicken strips, mixing to coat well.

2. Place the salad greens, cilantro (coriander), mint, scallions and grated lemongrass in a bowl; toss.

3. Heat the oil in a wok or large skillet. Add the chicken and stir-fry about for 2 minutes. Transfer to a plate and keep warm. Return the skillet to the heat and add the onion; sauté until soft. Add the tomatoes and cook, stirring briefly.

4. Return the chicken to the wok and heat until cooked through, about 5 minutes. Arrange the chicken, tomatoes and onion on top of the salad.

5. Return the wok to the heat and add the fish sauce, lime juice and sugar. Heat through, stirring to dissolve the sugar, then drizzle over the salad. Serve garnished with lemongrass slivers and herbs.

CHILI CHICKEN AND MANGO SALAD

Ingredients

$^1/_3$ cup / 50 g hazelnuts, finely chopped

$^1/_2$ tsp hot red pepper (chili) flakes

2 tbsp vegetable oil

1½ lb / 600-700 g skinless boneless chicken breasts

1 tbsp lemon juice

2 tbsp white wine vinegar

2 tbsp extra-virgin olive oil

Salt and freshly ground pepper

5 oz / 150 g spinach leaves

½ cucumber, thinly sliced

1 ripe mango, peeled and thinly sliced

Method

Prep and cook time: 25 min

1. Combine the chopped nuts with the pepper flakes and spread on a plate. One at a time, add the chicken breasts and lightly coat on all sides, pressing crumbs firmly to help them adhere.

2. Heat the vegetable oil in a skillet and fry the chicken until browned on all sides and cooked through, about 8 minutes. Transfer chicken to a plate and keep warm. Return the skillet to the heat and add the lemon juice, 2–3 tablespoons water, vinegar and olive oil; cook, stirring to loosen browned bits from the skillet, until slightly thickened. Season with salt and pepper.

3. Slice the chicken and arrange on plates with spinach, cucumber, and mango. Drizzle with the sauce and serve at once.

CHICKEN, BACON AND POTATO SALAD

Ingredients

For the potato salad:

1¾ lb / 800 g new potatoes, peeled and halved if large

2 tbsp walnut oil

4 tbsp vegetable oil

3 tbsp cider vinegar

1 tsp dry mustard

Salt and freshly ground pepper

½ bunch scallions (spring onions), thinly sliced

For the chicken:

4 skinless boneless chicken breasts, halved lengthwise

Salt and freshly ground pepper

1 tbsp olive oil

1 tsp butter

4 slices bacon

1 tbsp finely chopped fresh parsley

1 bunch watercress, trimmed

3–4 lettuce leaves, torn into bite-size pieces

Method

Prep and cook time: 50 min

1. Cook the potatoes in boiling salted water until tender, about 25 minutes. Drain and cut into bite-size pieces.

2. Whisk the oils, vinegar, mustard, salt and pepper in a large bowl. Add the potatoes and scallions (spring onions), mix well and let stand to absorb the flavors.

3. Meanwhile, heat the broiler (grill) and season the chicken with salt and pepper. Put under the broiler (grill) and cook thoroughly. Heat the oil and butter in a skillet and fry the bacon until crisp. Take out and drain on paper towels, leaving the fat in the skillet.

4. Arrange the potato salad on plates with the watercress and lettuce, add the chicken and bacon and serve.

SMOKED CHICKEN AND COUSCOUS SALAD

Ingredients

1½ cups / 250 g couscous

2 tbsp butter

3 cups / 350 g arugula (rocket)

1 small cucumber, sliced

1 radicchio lettuce, torn into bite-size pieces

1 red bell pepper, finely diced

12 oz / 350 g smoked chicken breast

Some fresh basil

Salad dressing

Salt and pepper

Method

Prep and cook time: 30 min

1. Pour hot water over the couscous as instructed on the packet, cover and let stand. Add the butter. Stir through the couscous with a fork and let cool.

2. Mix all the salad ingredients with the couscous and serve onto plates.

3. Slice the smoked chicken breast and arrange on the salad. Put a spoonful of salad dressing on each. Shred the basil and scatter over the salad. Season with salt and pepper and serve.

MAIN COURSES

WHOLE CHICKEN WITH APPLES

Ingredients

2 tbsp oil

1 chicken, about 3 lb / 1.5 kg

1 onion, cut into wedges

2 cups / 500 ml hard strong (dry) cider

2 tsp sugar

2 cups / 500 ml hot chicken broth (stock)

2 carrots, sliced

1 lemon, cut into wedges

4 apples

Salt and pepper

2 sprigs rosemary

Method

Prep and cook time: 2 hours

1. Heat the oven to 350 F (180C / Gas Mark 4).

2. Heat the oil in a skillet (frying pan) and put in the chicken breast side down. Cook for about 10 minutes, turning the chicken so that it browns all over.

3. Put the chicken, breast side down, in a large casserole dish. Set aside.

4. Add the onion wedges to the skillet and cook until golden. Pour in the cider and sugar and bring to a boil and then pour the hot cider mix over the chicken.

5. Cut the apples into wedges.

6. Add the hot broth (stock), carrots, lemon, apples, salt and pepper to the casserole dish. The chicken and vegetables should be covered by the liquid. Add the rosemary.

7. Cover and cook on high for 1-1½ hours until the chicken is cooked and the juices run clear when pierced with a skewer. Turn the chicken over about 20 minutes before the end of the cooking time.

CHICKEN LEGS WITH POTATOES AND SWEETCORN

Ingredients

4 chicken legs

1 tbsp honey

1 tsp sambal oelek or chile paste

1 tsp wine vinegar

2 lb / 900 g potatoes, peeled and cut into wedges

4 shallots, peeled and cut into wedges

4 tbsp vegetable oil

2 sprigs rosemary

1 cup / 200 g canned corn, drained and rinsed

Salt and freshly ground pepper

Method

Prep and cook time: 1 hour

1. Heat the oven to 350F (180 C / Gas Mark 4).

2. Mix together the honey, sambal oelek and vinegar and season with salt and pepper. Rub the mixture into the chicken legs.

3. Put the potatoes and shallots in a roasting pan and drizzle with the oil. Lay the chicken legs on top and scatter over the rosemary.

4. Roast in the oven for 20 minutes then baste the chicken with the juices and stir in the corn.

5. Return to the oven and cook for a further 20 minutes or until the juices from the meat runs clear.

ROSEMARY CHICKEN ON ROAST VEGETABLES

Ingredients

4 tbsp / 50 g butter, softened

1 medium chicken

2 tbsp chopped rosemary leaves

1 lemon, halved

3 tbsp vegetable oil

2 large carrots, peeled and sliced lengthways

4 small parsnips, peeled and sliced lengthways

6 new potatoes, scrubbed and sliced lengthways

12 garlic cloves, in their skins

Salt and freshly ground pepper

Rosemary sprigs, to garnish

Method

Prep and cook time: 1 hour 40 min

1. Heat the oven to 400F (200C / Gas Mark 6).

2. Rub the butter all over the chicken and sprinkle with salt and pepper. Scatter over half the rosemary leaves and put the remainder in the cavity along with the lemon halves.

3. Heat the oil in a roasting pan over a medium heat and add the vegetables, stirring so they are coated with the oil.

4. Place the chicken in the middle of the pan and roast in the oven for 20 minutes. Baste the meat, turn the vegetables and turn the heat down to 375F (190C / Gas Mark 5).

5. Roast for a further 30 minutes then baste again and add the garlic to the pan. Return to the oven and cook for another 30 minutes or until the meat juices run clear.

6. Serve garnished with rosemary sprigs.

CHICKEN LEGS WITH EGGPLANT AND LEMON

Ingredients

8 tbsp olive oil

1 tsp ground cumin

1 tsp paprika

1 tsp salt

Juice of 1 lemon

4 chicken legs

1 red onion, sliced

2 medium eggplants (aubergines), sliced

2 lemons, washed and sliced

Salt and freshly ground pepper

Cilantro (fresh coriander), to garnish

Method

Prep and cook time: 50 min

1. Heat the oven to 350F (180C/Gas Mark 4).

2. Mix 2 tbsp of the oil with the cumin, paprika, salt and lemon juice.

3. Separate the chicken thighs from the drumsticks, rub each piece with the cumin mixture and set aside.

4. Rub the sliced onions with a little oil and set aside.

5. Heat 2 tbsp oil in a ridged grill pan and grill the eggplant (aubergine) slices in batches for 1 minute on each side. Set aside and keep warm.

6. Heat the grill pan until smoking and sear the chicken pieces on all sides until lightly browned.

7. Put the chicken pieces in an ovenproof dish, tuck the eggplant, onion and lemon slices all around and drizzle with the remaining oil and the scrapings from the grill pan.

8. Season with salt and pepper and roast for 30 minutes, or until the chicken is cooked through, basting once. Serve garnished with cilantro (coriander) leaves.

ROAST CHICKEN ON CHICORY

Ingredients

8 small chicory heads

1 lb / 450 g Brussels sprouts

1 chicken, weighing about
3 lb 8 oz / 1.6 kg

Salt and pepper

1 sprig fresh thyme

1 sprig fresh rosemary

3 tbsp vegetable oil

1 garlic clove

½ cup / 125 ml dry white wine

Method

Prep and cook time: 1 hour 50 min

1. Preheat the oven to 400°F (200°C / Gas Mark 6). Trim the chicory heads and Brussels sprouts.

2. Season the chicken inside and out with salt and pepper. Strip the thyme and rosemary leaves from the stems. Put half the herbs inside the chicken cavity.

3. Heat the oil in a large roasting pan. Add the chicken and fry until golden brown on all sides.

4. Crush the garlic into the pan. Place the Brussels sprouts around the chicken. Pour in half of the wine.

5. Roast in the oven for 30–40 minutes, basting occasionally with the pan juices.

6. Add the chicory and the remaining wine to the pan. Sprinkle with the reserved herbs. Roast for a further 20–30 minutes until the chicken is cooked and the vegetables tender. The chicken is cooked when a skewer is inserted into the thickest part of the thigh and the juices run clear. Before serving, season to taste with salt and pepper.

CHICKEN LEGS
WITH APPLE

Ingredients

4 chicken legs

6 tbsp olive oil

2 tbsp honey

½ cup / 125 ml dry cider

12 shallots, peeled

4 dessert apples, cut into wedges and cored

Salt and freshly ground pepper

Sage leaves, to garnish

Method
Prep and cook time: 50 min

1. Heat the oven to 400 F (200C / Gas Mark 6).

2. Separate the chicken thighs from the drumsticks.

3. Heat the oil in a roasting pan and sear the chicken pieces until lightly browned on all sides. Remove from the pan and set aside.

4. Stir the honey and cider into the pan, let bubble then add the shallots. Stir for 2 minutes, season with salt and pepper then add the apples and coat them with the pan juices.

5. Return the chicken pieces to the pan, coat with the juices and cover with kitchen foil.

6. Roast in the oven for 30 minutes, or until the chicken is cooked through, basting frequently. Serve garnished with the sage leaves.

ROAST CHICKEN WITH RED ONIONS AND FENNEL

Ingredients

4 tbsp olive oil

2 large chicken legs, each cut into 3 pieces

2 tbsp black mustard seeds, lightly crushed

1 tsp black peppercorns, lightly crushed

2 carrots, peeled and cut into batons

2 red onions, cut into wedges

1 fennel bulb, trimmed and cut into wedges

8 sprigs thyme

1 cup / 250 ml white wine

Method

Prep and cook time: 1 hour

1. Heat the oven to 400°F (200°C / Gas Mark 6).

2. Heat the oil in a large skillet and brown the chicken pieces on all sides then transfer them to an ovenproof dish.

3. Return the skillet to the heat and add the mustard seeds and peppercorns. Cook over a high heat for 1 minute then scatter over the chicken pieces.

4. Tuck the carrots, onions and fennel wedges around the meat with the thyme sprigs, pour over the wine and cover with kitchen foil.

5. Roast in the oven for 20 minutes, basting once, then remove the foil, baste once more and return the dish to the oven for 10–15 minutes or until the chicken is cooked through and the vegetables are tender.

TERIYAKI CHICKEN

Ingredients

3 tbsp honey

6 tbsp teriyaki sauce

2 tbsp vegetable oil

1 chicken, trussed

For the salad:

4 oz / 100 g snow peas (mangetout)

2 tbsp rice vinegar

1 tbsp lemon juice

3 tbsp sesame oil

½ tsp salt

2 carrots, peeled and finely sliced lengthways

½ cucumber, peeled and finely sliced lengthways

1 cup / 100 g soya bean sprouts

Method

Prep and cook time: 2 hours plus 2 hours to marinate

1. Mix the honey with the teriyaki sauce and oil and brush the chicken with the mixture. Marinate for 2 hours.

2. Heat the oven to 400F, (200C / Gas Mark 6). Place the chicken on a rack in a roasting pan and roast for 20 minutes.

3. Turn the oven down to 350F (180C / Gas Mark 4), baste the chicken with the marinade and roast for a further 1 hour or until the chicken is cooked through, basting every 20 minutes.

4. Remove the chicken from the oven and rest for 15 minutes.

5. Blanch the snow peas (mangetout) in boiling water for 2 minutes. Drain, refresh in cold water and pat dry with kitchen paper.

6. Mix together the rice vinegar, lemon juice, sesame oil and salt and toss into the salad vegetables and snow peas.

7. Serve the chicken with the salad.

CHICKEN THIGHS WITH LEMON AND VEGETABLES

Ingredients

1 tbsp vegetable oil

1 tsp sweet paprika sweet

Salt and pepper

Juice of 1 lemon

8 chicken thighs

6 tbsp olive oil

1 onion, finely sliced

1 small zucchini (courgette), roughly chopped

1 small eggplant (aubergine), roughly chopped

2 new potatoes, scrubbed and halved

1 red bell pepper, roughly chopped

1 yellow bell pepper, roughly chopped

1 green bell pepper, roughly chopped

4 cloves garlic, unpeeled

½ cup / 125 ml vegetable broth (stock)

2 lemons, sliced

2 tbsp honey

Method

Prep and cook time: 50 min
plus 30 min to marinate

1. Mix the vegetable oil, paprika, salt, pepper and lemon juice and brush the chicken thighs with the mixture. Marinate for at least 30 minutes.

2. Heat the oven to 400°F (200°C / Gas Mark 6).

3. Heat 2 tbsp of the olive oil in a large ovenproof dish and brown the chicken thighs on all sides. Remove the meat from the pan and keep warm.

4. Heat the remaining oil in the pan and stir in the onion, zucchini (courgette), eggplant (aubergine), bell peppers, potatoes and garlic until all the vegetables are well coated.

5. Place the chicken thighs on top of the vegetables, pour over the broth (stock), season with salt and pepper then cover with kitchen foil and bake in the oven for 20 minutes, basting after 10 minutes.

6. Remove the foil and baste once more. Smear the lemon slices with the honey then lay on top of the chicken, drizzle over the remaining honey and return the dish to the oven for 10–15 minutes or until the chicken is cooked through.

CHICKEN WINGS IN HOISIN SAUCE

Ingredients

12 chicken wings

Salt and freshly ground pepper, to taste

1 tbsp honey

1 tbsp hoisin sauce

2 cloves garlic, minced

1 inch / 3-cm piece fresh ginger root, peeled and grated

To garnish:

1 tbsp sesame seeds

4 scallions (spring onions), chopped

1 lemon, cut into wedges

Method

Prep and cook time: 40 min plus 15 min to marinate

1. Pre-heat the oven to 350°F (180°C / Gas Mark 4).

2. Place the chicken wings in an ovenproof dish. Season with salt and pepper.

3. To prepare the sauce, in a small bowl, combine the honey, hoisin sauce, garlic and ginger with 3 tbsp water. Spread over the chicken wings and toss to coat. Let marinate for 15 minutes.

4. Roast the chicken for 30 minutes, brushing occasionally with the marinade, until well browned and cooked through. Serve at once, sprinkled with the sesame seeds and chopped scallions (spring onions) and garnished with lemon wedges.

CHICKEN WITH BACON AND ROOT VEGETABLES

Ingredients

2 carrots, peeled and cut into chunks

1 small celery root, peeled and cut into chunks

4 medium potatoes, peeled and cut into chunks

2 parsnips, peeled and cut into chunks

1 cup / 250 ml white wine

1 cup / 250 ml chicken broth (stock)

1 sprig thyme, chopped

1 sprig rosemary, chopped

3 garlic cloves, chopped

1 chicken, trussed

2 tbsp olive oil

3 slices bacon

Salt and freshly ground pepper

Method

Prep and cook time: 1 hour 45 min

1. Heat the oven to 400F (200C / Gas Mark 6).

2. Put the vegetables into a large roasting pan, pour over the wine and broth (stock) and scatter over the herbs and garlic.

3. Rub the chicken with the oil, season with salt and pepper and place on top of the vegetables. Lay the bacon slices over the chicken and cover with kitchen foil.

4. Roast in the oven for 1 hour, basting the chicken and turning the vegetables every 20 minutes.

5. Remove the foil and roast for a further 20 minutes or until the chicken is golden brown and cooked through. The chicken is cooked when a skewer is inserted into the thickest part of the thigh and the juices run clear.

6. Let the chicken rest for 15 minutes before serving

ROAST CHICKEN WITH BORLOTTI BEANS AND TORTIGLIONI

Ingredients

1 small chicken, trussed

4 tbsp / 50 g butter, softened

1 bunch thyme

4 oz / 100 g tortiglioni or pasta tubes

4 cups / 1 liter chicken broth (stock)

4 large scallions (spring onions), peeled and green parts removed

½ small green cabbage, chopped

8 oz / 200 g sugar snap peas

2 cups / 400 g canned borlotti beans, drained and rinsed

8 sun-dried tomatoes, chopped

1 tbsp chopped parsley

Salt and freshly ground pepper

Method

Prep and cook time: 1 hour 35 min

1. Heat the oven to 425F (220C / Gas Mark 7).

2. Rub the chicken all over with the butter, place in an ovenproof dish and season with salt and pepper. Chop a few of the thyme leaves and scatter over the chicken. Put the remaining thyme in the cavity of the chicken.

3. Roast the chicken in the oven for about 1¼ hours, basting from time to time. Turn the oven down to 350 F (180 C / Gas Mark 4) after 20 minutes.

4. Half an hour before the end of cooking time, cook the pasta according to the package instructions. Drain well and rinse.

5. Bring the broth (stock) to a boil in a large pan and add the scallions (spring onions). Let boil for 5 minutes then add the cabbage and sugar snap peas.

6. Boil for 2 minutes then add the borlotti beans, cooked pasta, tomatoes and parsley. Heat through then pour the vegetables into the dish with the chicken. Return to the oven for 10 minutes and serve.

ROAST LEMON CHICKEN

Ingredients

3 lemons

2 tbsp vegetable oil

Salt and pepper

1 large chicken

2 lb / 900 g small waxy potatoes

8 sprigs thyme

2 cups / 475 ml chicken broth (stock)

4 scallions (spring onions)

1 red bell pepper

1 tbsp honey

4 tsp sherry

Method

Prep and cook time: 1 hour 40 min

1. Preheat the oven to 375°F (190°C / Gas Mark 5). Remove the zest from 1 lemon and slice all the lemons.

2. Mix half the lemon zest with 1 tbsp of oil and salt and pepper. Rub the mixture all over the chicken. Tie the legs together with string and tuck the wings under the chicken.

3. Peel the potatoes and put in a roasting pan with the lemon slices. Place the chicken, breast side down, in the pan and add the thyme sprigs.

4. Roast in the oven for 30 minutes, occasionally pouring some of the chicken broth (stock) over the top and basting with the pan juices.

5. Meanwhile, cut the scallions (spring onions) into short lengths. Roughly chop the red pepper, discarding the core and seeds.

6. Remove the chicken from the pan and add the scallions and red pepper to the roasting pan.

7. Put the honey, sherry, remaining oil and lemon zest in a bowl and mix together. Return the chicken to the pan, breast side up, baste with the marinade and sprinkle with salt and pepper.

8. Roast the chicken for a further 35–45 minutes until golden brown. Check that the juices run clear before serving. Arrange the roast chicken, lemon slices and vegetables on a serving platter. Season the pan juices to taste and serve as a sauce.

CHICKEN WITH SWEET POTATOES AND CRANBERRIES

Ingredients

1 tbsp oil

3 lb / 1.5 kg corn fed chicken

1 red onion, sliced

1 garlic clove, chopped

5 sweet potatoes, peeled and cut into quarters

2 cups / 225 g cranberries

4 cups / 1 liter hot chicken broth (stock)

Salt and pepper

Some sprigs fresh rosemary

Method

Prep and cook time: 1 hour 50 min

1. Heat the oil in a skillet (frying pan) and fry the chicken, breast side down, for about 10 minutes until browned. Put the chicken in a casserole dish.

2. Fry the onion and garlic in the skillet until softened then put them into the dish with the chicken. Add the sweet potatoes and cranberries to the pan.

3. Season the broth (stock) with salt and pepper to taste and pour over the chicken. The chicken and vegetables should be covered with liquid. Tuck in the sprigs of rosemary.

4. Cover and cook for about 1-1½ hours until the chicken is thoroughly cooked and the vegetables are tender.

STICKY HONEY AND MUSTARD CHICKEN WINGS

Ingredients

4 tbsp thick honey

4 tbsp Dijon mustard

4 tbsp olive oil

1 tsp mustard seeds (optional)

Grated zest and juice of 2 lemons

12 chicken wings

Salt and pepper

1 scallion (spring onion), to garnish

Method

Prep and cook time: 1 hour

1. Put the honey, mustard, olive oil, mustard seeds, if using, the lemon zest and juice in a bowl and mix together.

2. Put the chicken wings into a large, non-metallic ovenproof dish and season with salt and pepper.

3. Drizzle over the honey and mustard mixture and stir to mix into the chicken wings. Cover and leave to marinate in the refrigerator for about 20 minutes.

4. Meanwhile, preheat the oven to 400°F (200°C / Gas Mark 6). Roast the chicken wings, basting occasionally, for 20–30 minutes until golden brown and thoroughly cooked through.

5. Meanwhile, shred the scallion (spring onion) and put into a bowl of cold water. Chill in the refrigerator to make the scallions curl.

6. Serve the chicken wings garnished with the scallion curls.

MOROCCAN CHICKEN WITH PUMPKIN

Ingredients

1 lb / 450 g pumpkin

1 lb / 450 g cherry tomatoes, on the vine

2 tbsp olive oil, plus extra to sprinkle

Salt and pepper

4 garlic cloves

1 cup / 35 g fresh cilantro (coriander) leaves

½ tsp paprika

½ tsp ground cumin

½ tsp curcuma (turmeric)

2 tbsp lemon juice

4 boneless chicken breasts, with skin on

Method
Prep and cook time: 1 hour

1. Preheat the oven to 350°F (180°C / Gas Mark 4).

2. Skin and cut the pumpkin into wedges, discarding the seeds, and put into an ovenproof dish with the tomatoes. Sprinkle with olive oil and season with salt and pepper.

3. Roughly chop the garlic. Put into a mortar with the cilantro (coriander) leaves, reserving a few to garnish, and the paprika, cumin, curcuma (turmeric), olive oil and lemon juice, and crush to a fine paste. Season with salt and pepper.

4. Rub the paste into the chicken breasts.

5. Place the chicken breasts on top of the vegetables, skin side up, and cook in the oven for about 30 minutes until golden brown and cooked through. Serve scattered with the reserved cilantro leaves.

ROAST CHICKEN WITH PORK, ONION AND SAGE STUFFING

Ingredients

6 oz / 150 g ground pork

1 cup / 50 g fresh breadcrumbs

1 small onion, finely chopped

2 tsp dried sage

Salt and pepper

1 medium chicken, trussed

1 stick / 100 g butter

Parsley, to garnish

For the vegetables:

1½ lb / 600 g small new potatoes, washed

3 tbsp olive oil

1 lb / 450 g carrots, cut into batons

8 oz / 200 g green beans, trimmed

½ stick / 50 g butter, melted

Method

Prep and cook time: 2 hours

1. Heat the oven to 375°F (190°C / Gas Mark 5).

2. Mix the pork, breadcrumbs, onion and sage, season with salt and pepper and stuff into the cavity of the chicken.

3. Smear the chicken with the butter, sprinkle with salt and place in a roasting pan.

4. Roast the chicken for about 1¾ hours, basting with the juices every 20 minutes or so. The chicken is cooked when a skewer is inserted into the thickest part of the thigh and the juices run clear. Rest the chicken for 15 minutes in a warm place before serving.

5. While the chicken is cooking, put the potatoes in a large pan of salted water and bring to a boil. Simmer for about 15 minutes or until the potatoes are just tender. Heat the oil in a skillet and sauté the potatoes until golden brown. Set aside and keep warm.

6. While the chicken is resting, steam or boil the carrots and green beans until tender. Drain well and coat with the melted butter. Serve the chicken and the vegetables sprinkled with chopped parsley.

THYME AND LEMON CHICKEN

Ingredients

1 chicken, about 2½ lb / 1.2 kg

10 sprigs thyme

3 tbsp olive oil

1 cup / 250 ml white wine

4 lemons

Salt and freshly ground pepper

Method

Prep and cook time: 1 hour

1. Preheat the oven to 350F (180C / Gas Mark 4). Divide the chicken into eight pieces.

2. Strip the leaves from half of the thyme sprigs. Put the leaves between the chicken skin and the meat. Season with salt and pepper.

3. Heat the oil in a roasting pan and brown the chicken on all sides. Pour in the white wine.

4. Quarter the lemons and add them to the pan along with the remaining thyme sprigs.

5. Roast for about 30 minutes, or until the chicken is cooked through, basting occasionally.

SPICY POUSSIN

Ingredients

4 poussins, each weighing about
1 lb / 450 g, or 2 spring chickens

Sea salt

4 garlic cloves, crushed

1 tbsp dried oregano

2 tsp paprika

1 tsp coarsely ground black pepper

Grated zest and juice of 2 lemons

4 tbsp olive oil

1¼ cups / 300 ml chicken
broth (stock)

2 tbsp balsamic vinegar

2 roasted red bell peppers

4 handfuls wild arugula (rocket)

½ cup / 50 g Parmesan cheese

8 tsp chili jam, to garnish

Method

Prep and cook time: 1 hour

1. Preheat the oven to 400°F (200°C / Gas Mark 6). Put the poussins in a large roasting pan and season with sea salt.

2. Sprinkle the garlic over the poussins with the oregano, paprika, black pepper and lemon zest. Drizzle over the lemon juice and olive oil.

3. Add the chicken broth (stock) and balsamic vinegar to the roasting pan, cover with foil and roast for 20 minutes (or 35 minutes for spring chicken).

4. Remove the foil, baste the birds with the juices and roast for a further 15 minutes until the birds are browned and thoroughly cooked through.

5. Meanwhile, cut the red peppers into quarters, discarding the cores and seeds.

6. Place the poussins on serving plates with some of the pan juices, each with 2 pepper quarters and a handful of arugula (rocket).

7. Using a vegetable peeler, shave the Parmesan cheese on top. Season with black pepper and serve garnished with chili jam.

CHICKEN WITH FORTY CLOVES OF GARLIC

Ingredients

4 chicken breasts, on the bone and skinned

Salt and pepper

5 tbsp olive oil

1 red onion, cut into wedges

6 sprigs thyme

4 bay leaves

1 lemon, sliced

40 garlic cloves, peeled

½ cup / 125 ml water

Method

Prep and cook time: 1 hour 50 min

1. Preheat the oven to 400°F (200°C / Gas Mark 6).

2. Generously season the chicken with salt and pepper.

3. Heat the oil in a large flameproof casserole. Add the chicken and onion and cook for 10 minutes, turning occasionally, until the chicken is browned on all sides.

4. Add the thyme, 2 bay leaves, lemon slices and garlic cloves, baste with the oil and meat juices and pour in the water.

5. Cover with a tight fitting lid and cook in the oven for 1½ hours until the chicken and garlic are very tender. Serve garnished with the remaining bay leaves.

CHICKEN MOLE

Ingredients

1 tbsp oil

4 boneless chicken thighs

4 chicken drumsticks

1 onion, chopped

3 garlic cloves

2 sticks celery, chopped

1 red bell pepper, deseeded and sliced

1 tsp chili powder

1 tsp ground cumin

1 tsp ground cinnamon

Pinch ground cloves

2 tbsp all purpose (plain) flour

2 x 14 oz / 400g cans chopped tomatoes

2 cups / 450 ml chicken broth (stock)

2 oz / 50 g dark chocolate (70% cocoa solids), chopped

Salt and pepper

Method

Prep and cook time: 45 min

1. Heat the oil in a skillet (frying pan) and fry the chicken pieces until browned on all sides. Remove from the pan and set aside.

2. Add the onion, garlic, celery and red bell pepper to the pan and fry for 5 minutes.

3. Add the spices and flour to the pan and cook for 2 minutes.

4. Stir in the tomatoes and broth (stock), then add the chocolate. Season to taste with salt and pepper. Bring to a boil.

5. Add the chicken to the sauce in the pan. Cover and simmer for about 25 minutes, until the chicken is tender.

CHICKEN AND CHICKPEA CURRY

Ingredients

Serves 6

8 boneless, skinless chicken thighs

1 tbsp oil

2 tbsp / 25 g butter

2 onions, finely chopped

4 garlic cloves, crushed

1 red chili, sliced and seeds discarded

1 tsp ground cumin

3 tsp cardamom seeds, crushed

1 tsp ground curcuma (turmeric)

2 tsp garam masala

1 tsp grated fresh ginger

1 tsp salt

2 bay leaves, crushed

1¹/₃ cups / 300 ml chicken broth (stock)

1 x 14 oz / 400 g can chickpeas

Cilantro (coriander) leaves, to garnish

Method

Prep and cook time: 50 min

1. Preheat the oven to 400F (200C / Gas Mark 6). Cut each thigh into 4 pieces. Heat the oil in a skillet (frying pan) and cook the chicken pieces until browned. Remove from the pan.

2. Add the butter to the pan and when hot add the onions, garlic and chili. Cook until just beginning to color, then add the spices and salt. Cook for 1 minute. Add the bay leaves and broth (stock) and bring to the boil. Stir in the chickpeas.

3. Place the chicken in a baking dish and pour over the onion mixture. Cook in the oven for about 30 minutes until the stew is bubbling and the chicken is thoroughly cooked.

4. Serve garnished with cilantro (coriander) leaves.

POT AU FEU

Ingredients

8 scallions (spring onions)

9 oz / 250 g asparagus

1 garlic clove

4 tbsp olive oil

1 chicken, cut into 8 pieces

1 tbsp thyme

2 bay leaves

^{2}/$_3$ cup / 200 ml chicken broth (stock)

1 lb / 450 g small potatoes

7 oz / 200 g small carrots

Salt and pepper

Method

Prep and cook time: 1 hour

1. Cut the scallions (spring onions) and asparagus into short lengths. Finely chop the garlic.

2. Heat the oil in a large skillet (frying pan), add the chicken pieces and fry until browned on all sides.

3. Add the garlic, thyme and bay leaves to the chicken, stir briefly, then add the broth (stock). Simmer gently for 30 minutes.

4. Add the scallions, asparagus, potatoes and carrots and simmer for a further 20 minutes until the vegetables are tender. Season to taste with salt and pepper before serving.

CURRIED CHICKEN WITH COCONUT SAUCE

Ingredients

4 shallots

2 garlic cloves

4 boneless chicken breasts, skinned

2 small red chilies

9 oz / 250 g snow (sugar snap) peas

1 tbsp vegetable oil

¾ cup / 200 ml coconut milk

2 tbsp panang curry paste

2 tbsp fish sauce

2 tbsp sugar

Snipped chives, to garnish

Method

Prep and cook time: 30 min

1. Finely chop the shallots and garlic. Cut the chicken breasts into cubes. Finely chop 1 of the chilies, discarding the seeds. Slice the other into thin rings, discarding the seeds. Cut the snow (sugar snap) peas in half.

2. Heat the oil in a wok. Add the shallots and garlic and fry for 1 minute.

3. Add the coconut milk, stir in the curry paste and simmer over a low heat for 2 minutes.

4. Add the cubed chicken, fish sauce, sugar and finely chopped chili. Cook over a low heat for a further for 3 minutes.

5. Add snow peas and continue to stir and fry for 5 minutes until the chicken is cooked through. Serve garnished with the chili rings and chives.

RATATOUILLE WITH CHICKEN

Ingredients

1 whole chicken, about 3 lb / 1.25kg (or chicken pieces)

Salt and pepper

Olive oil, for frying

2 red onions, cut into wedges

1 eggplant (aubergine), thickly sliced

2 zucchini (courgettes), thickly sliced

1 red bell pepper, sliced

2 cloves garlic, chopped in half

1 tsp tomato paste (purée)

¾–1 cup / about 200 ml chicken broth (stock)

1 tsp paprika

4 tomatoes, stems removed

Fresh basil leaves, to garnish

Method

Prep and cook time: 1 hour 15 min

1. Heat the oven to 350°F (180°C / Gas Mark 4).

2. Season the chicken pieces with salt and pepper and fry in hot oil in a flameproof casserole until golden brown. Remove and set aside.

3. Fry the onion, eggplant (aubergine) and zucchini (courgette). Sauté the bell peppers and the garlic, then add the tomato paste (purée) and pour in the broth (stock). Add the tomatoes and paprika and salt and pepper to taste.

4. Put the chicken pieces on top, skin side up and place in the oven for 30–40 minutes. Pour a little broth (stock) over the chicken from time to time and stir.

5. Adjust the seasoning with salt and pepper, sprinkle some basil leaves over the top and serve.

CHICKEN WITH ALMONDS

Ingredients

3 tbsp clarified butter or oil

1 onion, finely chopped

2 garlic cloves, finely sliced

1 tsp curcuma (turmeric)

4 chicken breasts, skinned and cut into chunks

½ cup / 125 ml chicken broth (stock)

½ cup / 125 ml heavy (double) cream

$^1/_3$ cup / 50 g ground almonds

4 pieces cinnamon

$^2/_3$ cup / 50 g flaked almonds, lightly toasted

2 tbsp chopped parsley

2 tbsp chopped cilantro (coriander) plus some to garnish

Salt and pepper

1 tsp paprika

Method
Prep and cook time: 30 min

1. Heat the butter in a large pan and gently fry the onion and garlic until soft.

2. Stir in the curcuma (turmeric), cook for 2 minutes then add the chicken and stir briefly. Pour over the chicken broth (stock) and cream and stir in the ground almonds and cinnamon.

3. Simmer very gently, stirring from time to time, for about 20 minutes or until the chicken is cooked through.

4. Stir in the flaked almonds and chopped herbs, season with salt and pepper and serve with the paprika sprinkled over and the cilantro (coriander) to garnish.

CHICKEN CASSOULET

Ingredients

4 chicken legs

2 lean pork belly rashers, diced

1 onion, chopped

2 garlic cloves, crushed

1 carrot, sliced

1 yellow bell pepper, deseeded
and sliced

2 tbsp all purpose (plain) flour

1 x 14 oz / 400 g can chopped
tomatoes

Scant 1 cup / 200 ml red wine

7 tbsp / 100 ml chicken broth (stock)

salt and pepper

2 x 14 oz / 400g cans navy (haricot)
beans, drained

4 oz / 100 g piece garlic sausage,
diced

1 bouquet garni

Rosemary, to garnish

Method

Prep and cook time: 1 hour 20 min

2. Heat a little oil in a skillet (frying pan) and
fry the chicken legs until browned all over.

3. Add the pork and onion to the pan and
cook for 5 minutes until lightly browned.
Add the garlic, carrot and bell pepper and
cook for 2 minutes.

4. Stir in the flour, followed by the tomatoes,
wine, broth (stock), salt and pepper. Bring to
a boil, stirring.

5. Put half the beans into the a casserole
dish. Place the chicken legs, garlic sausage
and bouquet garni on top.

6. Add the remaining beans, then pour in
the tomato mixture.

7. Cover and cook on low for 1 hour. Serve
garnished with rosemary

FRUITY MANGO CHICKEN

Ingredients

4 tbsp clarified butter or oil

8 chicken thighs, cut in half through the bone

4 onions, sliced

2 garlic cloves, crushed

Thumb-size piece fresh ginger, peeled and grated

1 tsp curcuma (turmeric)

1 tsp paprika

1 tsp ground cumin

1 tsp ground coriander

1 cup / 250 ml chicken broth (stock)

1 cup / 250 ml coconut milk

1 cup / 200 g mango chutney

Juice of 1 lemon

Salt and pepper

1 red chili pepper, deseeded and finely sliced

Method

Prep and cook time: 50 min

1. Heat the butter in a wide pan and cook the chicken pieces until lightly browned all over. Remove from the pan and set aside.

2. Gently fry the onions until soft but not brown then add the garlic, ginger, curcuma (turmeric), paprika, cumin and coriander. Fry for 2 minutes, stirring all the time.

3. Return the chicken to the pan, stir to coat in the spices then pour in the chicken broth (stock) and coconut milk. Simmer gently for 20 minutes then add the mango chutney and lemon juice and season with salt and pepper.

4. Let simmer for another 15 minutes or until the chicken is cooked through. Serve with the sliced chili scattered over.

PEARL BARLEY AND CHICKEN STEW

Ingredients

2 chicken breasts, skinned, cut into cubes

1 tbsp oil

1 onion, chopped

1 leek, sliced

4 carrots, thickly sliced

3 tbsp pearl barley rinsed

Salt and pepper

1 tsp chopped sage

2½ cups / 600 ml hot chicken broth (stock)

4 slices bacon, to garnish

Method

Prep and cook time: 1 hour 15 min

1. Heat the oil in a skillet (frying pan) and fry the chicken until browned on both sides. Remove from the pan and set aside.

2. Add the onions and leeks to the pan and fry gently for about 5 minutes until softened.

3. Add the carrots and cook for a further 4 minutes until they are beginning to soften.

4. Transfer the chicken and vegetables to a deep pan. Sprinkle the pearl barley over the top of the vegetables, season with salt, pepper and sage and pour in the broth (stock).

5. Bring to a boil and then cover and simmer for 30-40 minutes until the meat is tender and the barley is soft.

6. For the garnish, heat a skillet and fry the bacon until crisp on both sides. Drain on kitchen paper. Crumble over the top of the stew just before serving.

CURRIED CHICKEN LEGS WITH DATES AND MANGO

Ingredients

2 tbsp oil

1 tbsp garam masala

Salt

1 tbsp honey

Cayenne pepper

8 chicken legs (drumsticks)

1 cup mixed rice / 200 g (basmati and brown rice)

2½ cups / about 600 ml chicken broth (stock)

2 shallots

1 mango

1/3 cup / 50 g dried dates, roughly chopped

Curry powder: a good pinch of ginger, turmeric, cardamom, mace, nutmeg, cinnamon and cumin, all ground

1 tbsp parsley, chopped

1 tbsp mint, chopped

Mint leaves to garnish

Method

Prep and cook time: 45 min

1. Mix the oil with the garam masala, salt, honey and cayenne pepper and brush the chicken with the mixture. Put the chicken under a preheated broiler (grill) for about 30 minutes, turning occasionally, until cooked.

2. Meanwhile wash the rice, put into a pan with the chicken broth (stock) and bring to a boil.

3. Peel and chop the shallots and add to the rice.

4. Peel and halve the mango and remove the pit. Dice the flesh and add to the rice after about 20 minutes. Then add the dates and continue cooking gently for 5-10 minutes more, until done. Season with the curry powder, salt and cayenne pepper. Finally stir in the chopped parsley and mint.

5. Serve the chicken drumsticks in bowls on the rice and garnish with mint.

CHICKEN TIKKA MASALA

Ingredients

1 oven-ready chicken, 2½–3 lb / 1.2–1.4 kg

1 lemon

Salt & freshly milled pepper

For the marinade:

2 tsp freshly grated ginger

2 cloves garlic, pressed

2 cups / 500 g yogurt

2 tbsp vegetable oil

2 tbsp paprika

Spice mixture: ½ tsp ground cumin, black pepper, chili powder and curcuma (turmeric)

1 tbsp cilantro (coriander) leaves, chopped, to serve

Method

Prep and cook time: 1 hour 15 min plus 8 hours to marinate

1. Joint into the chicken into 6–8 pieces. Score the surface of the chicken pieces to a depth of ¼ inch (0.5 cm) and put into a shallow dish. Sprinkle with pepper, salt and the juice of a lemon. Let stand for about 30 minutes.

2. Mix all the spices for the marinade with the yogurt and the oil. Coat the chicken pieces generously with the marinade and seal the dish with aluminum foil. Marinate the chicken in the refrigerator for 8 hours or overnight.

3. Preheat the oven to 350°F (180°C / Gas Mark 4). Line a cookie sheet with aluminum foil and put the chicken pieces on the sheet. Cook in the oven for 35–40 minutes, brushing frequently with marinade (using about a quarter), and adding a little water if necessary.

4. Heat the remaining marinade in a large pan and add the chicken pieces. Continue to heat very gently for 5 minutes, then sprinkle with cilantro (coriander) and serve with rice.

CHICKEN STEW WITH CHANTERELLES

Ingredients

1 chicken, jointed (legs, wings, breast)

2 large scallions (spring onions)

14 oz / 400 g baking potatoes

2 carrots

2 parsnips

Salt & freshly milled pepper

2 tbsp olive oil

2 cloves garlic, peeled

1¼ cups / 300 ml chicken broth (stock)

1 bay leaf

7 oz / 200 g chanterelles

2 tbsp / 25 g butter

2 tbsp thyme leaves

a few fresh sage leaves

Method

Prep and cook time: 1 hour 15 min

1. Trim the scallions (spring onions) and cut into 2 inch (5 cm) lengths.

2. Peel the potatoes and dice finely, so that they will disintegrate and thicken the sauce.

3. Peel the carrots and parsnips and quarter lengthways.

4. Season the chicken pieces with salt and pepper, heat the oil in a large pan and brown the chicken pieces on all sides. Then add the vegetables, garlic and the broth (stock).

5. Add the bay leaf, cover and stew gently for about 1 hour. Stir frequently and add more broth if necessary.

6. Clean the chanterelles and sauté in butter. Remove from the heat.

7. Five minutes before the end of cooking time add the herbs and chanterelles to the stew. Check the seasoning of the sauce and serve.

RED CHICKEN CURRY

Ingredients

1 lb 6 oz / 600 g chicken breasts

3 tomatoes

1 cup / 200 g pineapple pieces

2 stalks lemongrass

1 tbsp oil

1¾ cups / 400 ml unsweetened coconut milk

1 tbsp brown sugar

3 tbsp fish sauce

2 tbsp lime juice

For the red curry paste:

About 1 inch / 2.5 cm galangal

1 shallot, peeled

1 clove garlic, peeled

About 1 inch / 2.5 cm lemongrass

2 Thai chilis

Zest of a kaffir lime

½–1 tsp shrimp paste

Salt

Method

Prep and cook time: 30 min

1. For the red curry paste place all the ingredients except for the shrimp paste and the salt in a mortar and finely crush. Now mix in the salt and the shrimp paste and stir until smooth.

2. Cut the chicken breasts into 1 inch (2.5 cm) pieces. Place the tomatoes into boiling water, then immediately into cold water. Peel, quarter, de-seed and chop the tomatoes. Chop the pineapple into small pieces. Wash and trim the lemongrass, then finely chop.

3. Heat the oil in a wok or skillet. Fry the curry paste, then pour in the coconut milk and bring to a boil. Season with lemongrass, sugar, fish sauce and lime juice. Add the chicken pieces and the pineapple and simmer for about 5 minutes. Now add the tomatoes and heat until cooked.

4. Divide into 4 bowls and serve.

FRUITY CHICKEN CURRY

Ingredients

2 tbsp vegetable oil

1 onion, chopped

1 carrot, cut into 8 sticks

1 clove garlic, crushed

2 boneless, skinless chicken breasts, cut into small chunks

1 tbsp korma curry paste

1 tbsp mango chutney

$^2/_3$ cups / 150 ml unsweetened coconut milk

1 eating apple, cored, quartered and roughly chopped

$^2/_3$ cup / 100 g frozen peas

To serve:

8 mini poppadums

Cooked basmati rice

Method

Prep and cook time: 30 min

1 Heat the oil in a skillet and gently fry the onion for a few minutes to soften (do not brown). Add the carrot and garlic and cook 1 minute more.

2 Add the chicken and stir-fry for a few minutes, to brown. Stir in the korma curry paste, mango chutney, coconut milk, apple and 150ml / $^2/_3$ cup of water. Bring to a boil, reduce heat and simmer for 8 minutes.

3 Add the peas and cook for a further 2 minutes. Serve with mini poppadums and rice.

BRAISED CHICKEN WITH VEGETABLES

Ingredients

1 medium-sized chicken

2 tbsp sunflower oil

1 onion, chopped

2 cloves garlic, chopped

2 sticks celery, chopped

2 carrots, sliced

1 lb / 450 g small potatoes

1 can chopped tomatoes (14 oz / 400 g)

1 cup / 250 ml chicken broth (stock)

Worcestershire sauce

8 oz / 250 g broccoli florets

5 oz / 150 g snow (sugarsnap) peas

1 handful spinach leaves, washed and drained

1¼ cups / 150 g frozen speas

2 tsp chopped thyme

Salt & freshly milled pepper

Method

Prep and cook time: 1 hour 30 min

1. Preheat the oven to 350°F (180°C / Gas Mark 4).

2. Fry the chicken in hot oil in a large flameproof casserole and remove.

3. Sauté the onions, garlic, celery, carrots and potatoes. Add the tomatoes and pour in the chicken broth (stock) and Worcestershire sauce.

4. Put the chicken inside the casserole, cover and cook in the oven for about 1 hour.

5. Take the chicken out of the pot and add the remaining vegetables. Cook for a further 10 minutes.

6. Remove the skin and bones from the chicken and cut into pieces. Put the chicken back in the casserole, sprinkle chopped thyme over the top and cook for a further 5 minutes, until the chicken is cooked though and the vegetables are tenders. Season to taste and serve.

CHICKEN CURRY (ASIAN STYLE)

Ingredients

3–4 chicken breast fillets
(1 lb 6 oz / 600 g)

2 tbsp sesame oil

2 cloves garlic, chopped

1 tsp freshly chopped ginger

Scant 1 cup / 200 ml unsweetened coconut milk

1 tbsp tomato paste (tomato purée)

2 tsp red curry paste

Scant ½ cup / 100 ml vegetable broth (stock)

1 lb 2 oz / 500 g tomatoes

Juice of ½ lemon

2 sprigs Thai basil, shredded

2 sprigs cilantro (coriander), shredded

Salt & freshly milled pepper

Method

Prep and cook time: 30 min

1. Cut the chicken breast fillets into strips approximately ½–¾ inches (1.5–2 cm) wide.

2. Heat the sesame oil in a wok or skillet and fry the chicken, garlic and ginger for 3–4 minutes.

3. Then stir in the coconut milk, tomato paste (tomato purée), curry paste and vegetable broth (stock) and simmer for a further 4 minutes or so.

4. Drop the tomatoes into boiling water for a few seconds, refresh in cold water, then skin, quarter, deseed and cut into wedges. Add to the chicken curry shortly before the end of cooking time.

5. To serve, stir the shredded basil and cilantro (coriander) leaves into the curry, season with salt and pepper and add lemon juice to taste. Serve in bowls accompanied by rice.

CHICKEN CHILI

Ingredients

Oil, for frying

1 onion, finely chopped

1 clove garlic, finely chopped

1 tsp chili powder, or more, according to taste

1 potato, peeled and finely diced

2 chicken breasts, skinned and chopped

1 red bell pepper, deseeded and chopped

1 can red kidney beans, drained and rinsed

14 oz / 400 g can tomatoes, chopped

2 tsp Worcestershire sauce

2 bay leaves

Thyme leaves, to garnish

Method
Prep and cook time: 30 min

1. Heat the oil in a large pan and gently cook the onion until soft but not brown. Add the garlic, cook for 1 minute then sprinkle in the chili powder.

2. Stir well then add the potato and chicken breasts and cook gently for 2 minutes. Add the bell pepper, kidney beans, tomatoes, Worcestershire sauce and bay leaves. Season with salt and pepper and let simmer for 20 –25 minutes.

3. Serve with thyme leaves to garnish.

CHICKEN KORMA

Ingredients

1 lb 2 oz / 500 g chicken breast fillet

1 sachet saffron

Good ¾ cup / 200 g plain yogurt

For the spice mixture:

2 onions

3 cloves garlic

2 red chilis

1 tsp freshly grated ginger

½ cup/50 g ground almonds

In addition:

2 tbsp ghee or clarified butter

A good pinch of ground cardamom

½ tsp ground cinnamon

1½ tsp ground cumin

1½ tsp ground coriander

1–2 lime leaves

2 curry leaves

1¾ cups / 400 ml unsweetened coconut milk

Salt

Sugar

2 tbsp chopped almonds

Chopped celery, to garnish

Method

Prep and cook time: 1 hour 15 mins plus 4 hours to marinate

1. Cut the chicken into bite-size pieces. Dissolve the saffron in 1 tablespoon hot water and mix with the yogurt. Add the chicken pieces and marinate for about 4 hours.

2. Peel and finely chop the onions and garlic. Trim the chilis, removing the seeds if you wish, and cut into rings. Mix together the onions, garlic, chili, grated ginger and ground almonds.

3. Melt the ghee or clarified butter in a pan, add the cardamom, cinnamon, cumin and coriander and sauté briefly. Then add the prepared onion and spice mixture, the lime leaves and curry leaves and sauté, stirring, for 2–3 minutes. Now add the coconut milk and the meat with the marinade and cook for about 45 minutes. Season with salt and sugar, stir in the chopped almonds and spoon into bowls.

4. Serve sprinkled with chopped celery.

SPICED CHICKEN WITH COUSCOUS

Ingredients

8 boneless chicken thighs, each cut into 3

Salt and pepper

2 tsp medium curry powder

2 tsp paprika

½ tsp ground cinnamon

5 tbsp olive oil

1 onion, chopped

5 cloves garlic, crushed

14 oz / 400 g canned tomatoes

1 cup / 150 g dried apricots, chopped

2 cups / 375 g couscous

2 cups / 450 ml hot vegetable broth (stock)

4 tbsp / 50 g butter, diced

2 tbsp chopped parsley

4 tbsp toasted flaked almonds

Method

Prep and cook time: 45 min
plus 30 min to marinate

1. Put the chicken into a large bowl and season generously with salt and pepper.

2. Mix together the curry powder, paprika, cinnamon and 3 tbsp of olive oil. Spoon over the chicken and turn to coat all over. Cover and marinate for 30 minutes.

3. Heat the oven to 400F (200 C / Gas Mark 6).

4. Heat an ovenproof dish over a medium flame with the remaining oil and cook the chicken for 10 minutes until browned all over. Add the chopped onion and garlic and cook for a further 2 minutes.

5. Add the tomatoes and apricots, bring to a boil then cover the dish and cook in the oven for 20 minutes until the chicken is cooked through.

6. Meanwhile, put the couscous into an heatproof dish. Pour on the hot vegetable broth (stock) and add 1 tsp salt. Stir, leave for 10 minutes until the broth has been absorbed then fluff up with a fork. Dot the butter over the couscous and keep warm.

7. Stir the parsley into the spiced chicken, garnish with toasted flaked almonds and serve with the couscous alongside.

GREEN CHICKEN CURRY

Ingredients

For the green curry paste:

2 scallions (spring onions), trimmed

2 red chili peppers, deseeded and roughly chopped

2 cloves garlic, peeled

1 walnut-sized piece fresh ginger, peeled and grated

1 tsp coriander seeds, crushed

Salt & freshly milled pepper

1 stalk lemongrass, peeled and finely chopped

1 cup / 20 g Thai basil leaves

1 cup / 20 g cilantro (coriander) leaves

3 tbsp olive oil

1 lime, zest and juice

For the chicken:

4 chicken breasts, cut into bite-size pieces

Oil for frying

1¾ cups / 400 ml unsweetened coconut milk

2 tbsp chopped pistachios

2 kaffir lime leaves

1 red chili peppers, deseeded and thinly sliced

1 cup / 20 g cilantro (fresh coriander) leaves

Method
Prep and cook time: 30 min plus 30 min to marinate

1. Place all ingredients for the green curry paste in a blender and process to a coarse paste.

2. Marinate the chicken for about 30 minutes with some of the curry paste. Remove from the marinade and fry in a hot wok in oil for about 4 minutes.

3. Stir in the remaining curry paste, cook for 2 minutes then pour in the coconut milk.

4. Add the pistachios, the kaffir lime leaves, red chili peppers and cilantro leaves. Bring to a boil, then simmer gently for about 25 minutes. Season to taste with salt and serve with rice.

THAI CHICKEN CURRY

Ingredients

For the curry paste:

1 bunch scallions (spring onions), trimmed

3 medium size green chilies, deseeded and roughly chopped

2 cloves garlic, peeled

2 tsp freshly chopped ginger

2 tsp coriander seeds, crushed

Salt & freshly milled pepper

2 stalks lemongrass, peeled and finely chopped

½ bunch basil

1 bunch cilantro (coriander) leaves

3 tbsp olive oil

2 unwaxed lemons, zest and juice

For the curry:

4 chicken legs

1 stalk lemongrass

2 shallots

2 cloves garlic

7 oz / 200 g green baby eggplants (aubergine)

2 tbsp oil

4 kaffir lime leaves

1 tsp ginger, freshly grated

1 tbsp brown sugar

Fish sauce

1¼ cups / 300 ml coconut milk

1¾ cups / 400 ml chicken broth (stock)

Salt

Cilantro (coriander) or basil leaves, to garnish

Method
Prep and cook time: 30 min

1. Place all the ingredients for the curry paste in a blender and process to a smooth paste.

2. Skin, bone and dice the chicken legs. Slice the lemongrass very thinly. Peel and thinly slice the shallots and garlic.

3. Heat the oil in a wok and sauté the chicken for 1–2 minutes, until golden brown. Add 2 tbsp of the curry paste, then mix in the lemongrass, shallots, garlic, kaffir lime leaves, ginger and sugar. Sauté briefly, then stir in the coconut milk and chicken broth (stock). Add the eggplants and simmer gently for about 15 minutes. Add fish sauce and salt to taste. Serve sprinkled with herbs.

CREAMY CHICKEN CURRY

Ingredients

3 tbsp clarified butter or oil

1 onion, finely chopped

Thumb-size piece ginger, peeled and grated

2 garlic cloves, chopped

2 cloves, crushed

1 dried chili pepper, crushed

2 cardamom pods, crushed

1 tsp ground cumin

4 chicken breasts, skinned and cut into chunks

½ cup / 75 g ground almonds

1 cup / 250 ml chicken broth (stock)

½ cup / 125 ml heavy (double) cream

Salt and pepper

1 tbsp chopped cilantro (coriander) leaves

Method

Prep and cook time: 30 min

1. Heat the clarified butter in a large skillet and gently fry the onion, ginger and garlic until soft.

2. Stir in the crushed cloves, chili, cardamom and cumin and cook for 2 minutes, stirring all the time.

3. Add the chicken, brown the meat on all sides then stir in the almonds, chicken broth (stock) and cream. Simmer very gently for about 20 minutes or until the chicken is cooked through and the sauce is thick and creamy. Season to taste with salt and pepper.

4. Serve the korma with the rice and scatter over the cilantro (coriander).

CURRIED CHICKEN WITH BROCCOLI

Ingredients

For the curry paste:

1 red chili

1 clove garlic

¾ inch / 2 cm galangal, peeled

Good pinch grated zest of 1 kaffir lime

1 tsp shrimp paste

For the chicken dish:

4 chicken breasts

1 red onion

2 scallions (spring onions)

2 orange and red bell peppers

1 lb 2 oz / 500 g broccoli

2 tbsp oil

¾ –1 cup / 200 ml coconut milk

¾–1 cup / 200 ml chicken broth (stock)

1 tbsp ginger, freshly grated

1 lime

Soy sauce

Salt & freshly milled pepper

Method
Prep and cook time: 30 min

1. Cut the chicken into strips. Put all the curry paste ingredients except the shrimp paste into a mortar and grind to a paste. Then mix in the shrimp paste.

2. Peel, halve and slice the onion. Trim the scallions (spring onions) and cut into thin rings. Halve and core the bell peppers and cut into strips. Chop the broccoli into florets.

3. Heat the oil and sauté the onion, broccoli and bell peppers. Add 2 tablespoons of the curry paste and the scallions and sauté briefly, then add the coconut milk and chicken broth (stock). Simmer for 2–3 minutes.

4. Stir in the chicken and ginger and cook for 8–10 minutes, stirring occasionally, until the chicken is done.

5. Halve the lime, cut one half into wedges and squeeze the other half. Season the sauce with salt and pepper and add lime juice and soy sauce to taste. Serve on plates and garnish with the lime wedges.

CHICKEN AND CHORIZO CHILI

Ingredients

2 chicken breasts

2 slices (rashers) bacon

3½ oz / 100 g chorizo, Spanish spiced pork sausage

1 can kidney beans (14 oz / 400 g)

1 can cannellini beans (14 oz / 400 g)

2 red onions

2 cloves garlic

1 tbsp olive oil

1 tbsp tomato paste (purée)

1¾ cups / 400 ml meat broth (stock)

1 tbsp paprika, noble sweet

Salt & freshly milled pepper

Cayenne pepper

Pinch of dried oregano

4 tbsp sour cream

Method

Prep and cook time: 1 hour

1. Thinly slice the chicken breasts. Cut the bacon into strips. Thinly slice the chorizo.

2. Rinse and drain the beans. Peel and dice the onions and garlic.

3. Heat the oil and sauté the chicken, bacon and chorizo. Add the garlic and half of the onions and stir in the tomato paste (purée).

4. Stir in a little broth (stock). Add the paprika and simmer for about 20 minutes, stirring occasionally. Keep adding a little more broth (stock).

5. Then add the beans and simmer for a further 20 minutes or so. Season to taste with salt, pepper and cayenne pepper.

6. Spoon into bowls, scatter with the rest of the onion and sprinkle with a little oregano. Add a spoonful of sour cream to each serving. Serve with tortilla.

BUTTER CHICKEN

Ingredients

½ cup / 125 ml yogurt

3 tbsp ground almonds

2–3 tsp garam masala

1 pinch Indian five-spice powder

1 pinch cinnamon

1 cardamom pod, crushed

1 tsp ground ginger

2 garlic cloves, crushed

1 cup / 200 g canned tomatoes, chopped

1 tsp salt

4 medium chicken breasts, skinned and chopped into bite-size chunks

3 tbsp clarified butter or oil

1 onion, finely chopped

½ cup / 125 ml coconut milk

½ cup / 125 ml vegetable broth (stock) or water

2 handfuls spinach, washed

Salt and pepper

Method

Prep and cook time: 40 min plus 3 hours to marinate

1. Mix the yogurt, ground almonds, garam masala, five-spice, cinnamon, cardamom, ginger, garlic, tomatoes and salt.

2. Put the chicken into a large bowl and pour the yogurt sauce over it. Mix and leave to stand in a cool place for at least 3 hours.

3. Heat the butter in a deep skillet, add the onions and cook for 5 minutes.

4. Add the chicken and yogurt mixture, coconut milk and vegetable broth (stock). Bring to a boil then simmer over a low heat for 20 minutes or until the chicken is cooked through and the sauce has thickened.

5. Stir in the spinach and cook very gently for 5 minutes. Season to taste with salt and serve.

CHICKEN KERALA

Ingredients

6 tbsp oil

2 red onions, finely sliced

16 curry leaves

1 white onion, finely chopped

2 garlic cloves, chopped

Thumb-size piece ginger, peeled and finely chopped

1 tsp curcuma (turmeric)

1 tsp garam masala

2 red chili peppers, deseeded and finely chopped

1 tsp mustard seeds, crushed

1 tsp coriander seeds, crushed

4 cloves, crushed

1 tsp peppercorns, crushed

1 tsp salt

4 chicken breasts, skinned and cut into chunks

½ cup / 125 ml chicken broth (stock)

½ cup / 125 ml coconut milk

Method
Prep and cook time: 45 min

1. Heat the oil in a large skillet and gently fry the red onions until crisp but not burnt. Remove from the skillet and set aside.

2. Fry the curry leaves for 2 minutes then set aside.

3. Fry the white onion gently until soft but not brown then add the garlic, ginger, curcuma (turmeric), garam masala, chili peppers, mustard seeds, coriander seeds, cloves, peppercorns and salt.

4. Fry the mixture for 2 minutes then add the chicken. Stir briefly then pour in the chicken broth (stock) and coconut milk. Simmer gently, stirring from time to time, for 20 minutes or until the chicken is cooked through.

5. Serve with the fried red onions scattered over and the curry leaves to garnish.

CHICKEN WITH CHILIES AND BASIL

Ingredients

1 tbsp sesame oil

4 chicken breasts, cut into bite-size pieces

2 shallots, sliced

2 chilies, deseeded and sliced into thin strips

Fish sauce

Light soy sauce

½ bunch Thai basil, for garnish

Method

Prep and cook time: 20 min

1. Heat the oil and brown the meat on all sides. Add the shallots and sauté until translucent.

2. Add the chilies and soy sauce and fish sauce to taste, then cook over a very low heat until the meat is cooked through. Finally mix in the basil leaves and serve in bowls.

MOROCCAN CHICKEN WITH COUSCOUS

Ingredients

Around 2 lb / 1 kg chicken breast fillets

Zest and juice of 1 lemon

2 cloves garlic, finely chopped

4 tbsp olive oil

Salt & freshly milled pepper

2–3 tsp Moroccan spice mixture: paprika, cumin, curcuma (turmeric), ground coriander, cayenne pepper and saffron

For the yogurt dip:

1 cup / 250 ml whole-milk yogurt

Salt

1 pinch Moroccan spice mixture

For the couscous:

1¼ cups / 250 g couscous

Juice of 1 lemon

7 oz / 200 g ripe tomatoes, chopped

1 onion, finely chopped

1 small eggplant (aubergine), diced

1½ red bell peppers, deseeded and diced

1 tbsp olive oil

Freshly milled pepper

1 tbsp white wine vinegar

1 bunch cilantro (coriander)

Method
Prep and cook time: 50 min plus 3 hours marinating time

1. Remove any skin or fat from the meat. Cut the meat into 12 long thin strips.

2. Mix 2 tbsp lemon juice and 2 tbsp olive oil with the garlic, half of the lemon zest, salt, pepper, and the Moroccan spice mixture. Add the chicken, mix well, cover, and marinate in the refrigerator for about 3 hours.

3. Mix the yogurt and add the spices and salt to taste. Soak the wooden skewers in enough water to cover for 30 minutes (to prevent burning).

4. Cook the couscous according to the package instructions.

5. Put the lemon juice into a bowl and add the vegetables.

6. Heat a little of the oil in a skillet and sauté the mixed vegetables until they are softened. Stir in the vinegar and mix the vegetables with the couscous along with the cilantro (coriander). Check the seasoning.

7. Preheat the broiler (grill). Thread the pieces of chicken on wooden skewers. Sprinkle the chicken with the rest of the oil and broil (grill) on all sides until the chicken in thoroughly cooked.

8. Spoon the couscous onto plates or into dishes, add chicken skewers and a little yogurt sauce to each and serve.

CHICKEN IN SPICY COCONUT

Ingredients

2 cloves garlic, finely chopped

1 chili, sliced (wear gloves to prevent irritation)

1 tsp freshly grated ginger

1¾ cups / 200 ml coconut milk

Zest and juice of 1 lime

4 chicken breasts, diced

Wooden skewers

Sesame oil

Salt & freshly milled pepper

Method

Prep and cook time: 20 min plus
12 hours to marinate

1. Mix the garlic, ginger, chili, coconut milk, lime juice and zest to make a marinade and then mix with the diced chicken. For the best results put into a plastic bag so that everything is well covered and marinate in the refrigerator overnight.

2. Soak the wooden skewers in enough water to cover for 30 minutes (to prevent burning). Preheat the broiler (grill). Take the chicken out of the marinade, thread onto wooden skewers, sprinkle with a little oil and season with salt and pepper. Grill for 4–5 minutes, until cooked, turning occasionally.

CHICKEN AND PEACH SKEWERS

Ingredients

1 lb 4 oz / 600 g skinless boneless chicken breast, cut into bite-size chunks

2 peaches, pitted and diced

1 red bell pepper, cut into bite-size pieces

Vegetable oil, for brushing

1 tbsp oil

1 small chili pepper, chopped (wear gloves to prevent irritation)

1 garlic clove, chopped

1 mango, pitted and finely chopped

1 tsp honey

Light soy sauce, to taste

Fish sauce, to taste

Sea salt, to taste

Hot red pepper flakes, to taste

Method

Prep and cook time: 30 min plus 30 min soaking time

1. Preheat the grill or broiler. Soak 8 wooden skewers in water to cover for 30 minutes (to prevent burning).

2. Thread the chicken, peaches and bell pepper pieces onto the skewers, alternating them as you go. Brush with oil and grill or broil, turning frequently, for about 6-8 minutes or until the chicken is cooked through. Set aside and keep warm.

3. Meanwhile, to prepare the dip, heat the oil in a small skillet, add the chili and garlic and sauté briefly. Add the mango and honey and a little water; bring to a boil and cook, scraping browned bits from the skillet. Add soy sauce and fish sauce to taste and remove from the heat.

4. Put the chicken and peach skewers on plates, drizzle with a little of the dip and sprinkle with salt and pepper flakes. Serve the dip separately in a small bowl.

CURRIED CHICKEN SKEWERS WITH RAITA

Ingredients

For the skewers:

1 garlic clove, finely chopped

2 tsp curcuma (turmeric)

1 tsp curry powder

2 tbsp oil

Juice of ½ lime

4 chicken breasts, skinned and cut into chunks

For the raita:

1 cup / 250 ml yogurt

½ cucumber, deseeded and chopped

2 mint sprigs, leaves chopped

1 green chili pepper, chopped

1 tsp salt

Lime wedges, to garnish

Method

Prep and cook time: 20 min plus 2 hours marinating time

1. Mix together the garlic, curcuma (turmeric), curry powder, oil and lime juice. Mix in the chicken chunks and leave to marinate for 2 hours.

2. For the raita, mix togther all the ingredients and set aside.

3. Heat the broiler (grill) to a medium setting. Thread the chicken onto wooden skewers and broil (grill) for about 6 minutes, turning from time to time, or until the chicken is cooked through.

4. Serve the skewers with the raita and garnish with lime wedges.

CHICKEN WITH GINGER COCONUT SAUCE

Ingredients

8 chicken legs

3 tbsp oil

1 tsp spice mixture, (equal parts of ground ginger, black and white pepper, cayenne pepper)

3 shallots, finely diced

2 garlic cloves, finely chopped

1 tsp ginger, freshly grated

2 chilies, finely chopped

2/3 cup / 150 ml white wine

1 cup / 240 ml coconut milk

1 tbsp honey

8 oz / 225 g tub of crème fraîche

Salt & freshly milled pepper

1 tbsp fish sauce

2 tbsp cilantro (coriander), chopped

Kebab skewers

Method

Prep and cook time: 40 min

1. Skin the chicken legs, take the meat off the bone and dice.

2. Mix 2 tablespoons of oil with the spice mixture and mix with the chicken. Cover and chill.

3. Meanwhile, heat the rest of the oil and sauté the shallots and garlic without browning. Stir in the ginger and chili, then add the white wine.

4. Boil until reduced, then add the coconut milk, honey and crème fraîche and simmer, stirring occasionally, to produce a creamy sauce. Strain through a sieve, add the cilantro (coriander) and add seasoning and fish sauce to taste.

5. Thread the chicken onto skewers and fry or grill for about 5–6 minutes, turning frequently, until cooked. Put on plates and pour the sauce over.

CHICKEN AND NECTARINE SKEWERS

Ingredients

4 boneless chicken breasts, skinned

3 nectarines

3 scallions (spring onions)

2 tbsp olive oil

Salt and pepper

4 tbsp runny honey

Baby spinach leaves, to garnish

Method

Prep and cook time: 30 min

1. Cut the chicken into bite-size pieces. Cut the nectarines in half, remove the pits (stones) and cut the flesh into wedges. Slice the scallions (spring onions) diagonally, into 4 cm / 1½ inch pieces.

2. Thread the chicken pieces, nectarines and scallions on to wooden skewers. Brush with the oil and season with salt and pepper.

3. Preheat the broiler (grill). Cook the kebabs, turning frequently, for 6–8 minutes or until the chicken is cooked through. Baste with the honey during the last few minutes of the cooking time.

4. Arrange the leaves on serving plates and place the kebabs on top to serve.

CHICKEN SATAY

Ingredients

1 red chili, deseeded and finely chopped

1 shallot, finely chopped

2 garlic cloves, crushed

¼ tsp ground caraway

¼ tsp ground coriander

2 tbsp light soy sauce

4 tbsp coconut milk

2 tbsp vegetable oil

4 boneless chicken breasts, skinned

For the peanut sauce:

5 oz / 150 g unsalted, shelled peanuts

¾ cup / 200 ml coconut milk

2 tbsp peanut butter

1 tsp curry powder

1 lemon, zest and juice

2–3 tsp brown sugar

3 tbsp whipping cream

Method

Prep and cook time: 1 hour plus 1 hour to marinate

1. Put all the vegetables in a large bowl.

2. Add the caraway, coriander, soy sauce, coconut milk and oil and mix together to make a marinade.

3. Slice the chicken breasts into ¾ inch (2 cm) wide strips. Add to the marinade and leave for at least 1 hour. Remove the chicken from the marinade and shake off any excess.

4. Thread the chicken strips on to wooden skewers so they make a wavy shape.

5. Heat the broiler (grill) and cook the skewers for about 10 minutes, turning and basting occasionally with the marinade, until cooked through.

6. Meanwhile, to make the peanut sauce, toast the peanuts in a dry skillet (frying pan). Allow to cool and then crush finely in a mortar.

7. Put the coconut milk, peanut butter and curry powder in a saucepan and bring to the boil.

8. Mix the lemon zest and juice into the sauce. Season to taste with the sugar. Add the cream to the sauce and serve with the chicken skewers.

TANDOORI CHICKEN KEBABS

Ingredients

4 boneless chicken breasts, skinned

Salt and pepper

Juice of 1 lemon

2 garlic cloves

1 walnut-sized piece fresh ginger

1 cup / 200 g plain yogurt

2 tbsp vegetable oil

¼ tsp ground cumin

¼ tsp ground nutmeg

¼ tsp ground coriander

¼ tsp black pepper

¼ tsp paprika

For the raita:

1 cucumber

1¼ cups / 250 g plain yogurt

1 tbsp finely chopped fresh parsley

1 tbsp finely chopped fresh mint

½ tsp ground caraway

½ tsp ground coriander

Salt and pepper

Mint leaves, to garnish

Method

Prep and cook time: 40 min plus 12 hours marinating and 1 hour standing time for the raita

1. Cut the chicken into bite-size pieces and put in a shallow dish. Season with salt and pepper and drizzle over the lemon juice.

2. To make the marinade, crush the garlic. Peel and grate the ginger. Put in a bowl, add the yogurt, oil and the spices, and mix together.

3. Generously brush the chicken with the marinade and cover the dish with foil. Leave to marinate in the refrigerator overnight.

4. To make the raita, peel, remove the seeds from and grate the cucumber. Put in a bowl,

add the yogurt, parsley, mint, caraway and coriander, and season to taste with salt and pepper. Leave to stand for 1 hour.

5. Preheat the broiler (grill) and cover the rack with foil. Skewer the chicken pieces on to kebab sticks, reserving the marinade.

6. Cook the kebabs for about 8–10 minutes, turning halfway through the cooking time and brushing with the reserved marinade.

7. Serve the tandoori chicken kebabs with the raita, garnished with mint leaves.

CHICKEN KEBABS WITH COUSCOUS SALAD

Ingredients

1½ cups / 250 g couscous

1 lb / 450 g skinless boneless chicken breasts, cut into wide strips

Salt & freshly ground pepper

Juice of 1 lemon, divided

1 small zucchini (courgette), finely diced

2 tomatoes, finely diced

1 (14-oz) can / 400 g chickpeas, rinsed and drained

1 bunch parsley, finely chopped

4 radicchio lettuce leaves

Lemon wedges, to garnish

Cherry tomatoes, to garnish

Method

Prep and cook time: 35 min

1. Soak 12 wooden skewers in enough water to cover them for 20 minutes (to prevent burning). Preheat the broiler (grill).

2. Cook the couscous according to the instructions on the packet.

3. Meanwhile, thread the chicken strips onto the skewers. Season with salt and pepper and sprinkle with lemon juice, reserving 2 tablespoons. Marinate for 10 minutes.

4. Broil (grill) the kebabs for about 10 minutes, turning once, until browned and cooked through.

5. Meanwhile, combine the zucchini (courgette), tomatoes, chickpeas and parsley with the couscous; season with salt, pepper and the reserved lemon juice. Fill the radicchio leaves with the couscous salad and arrange on plates with the chicken kebabs and lemon wedges. Garnish with tomatoes.

CHICKEN WITH LIME BUTTER

Ingredients

12 oz / 350 g carrots, sliced

7 oz / 200 g snow peas (mangetout), trimmed

2 garlic cloves

2 tbsp lime juice

1 tsp lime zest

6 tbsp / 75 g soft butter

4 chicken breast fillets (skinned)

Salt & freshly milled pepper

Some basil leaves, shredded

Lime slices, to garnish

Method

Prep and cook time: 30 min

1. Blanch the carrots in boiling, salted water for 3–4 minutes, then drain, refresh in cold water, and drain thoroughly.

2. Peel the garlic. Mix the lime juice and zest with 4 tbsp (50 g) of the butter. Crush the garlic into the butter and season with a little salt. Mix well.

3. Season the chicken with salt and pepper. Put into a baking dish and spread with the garlic and lime butter. Cook under a preheated broiler (grill) for 5–10 minutes each side.

4. To serve, heat the vegetables in the rest of the butter and season with salt and pepper. Scatter the vegetables with basil and put on plates with the chicken breasts. Serve at once, garnished with lime slices.

PROSCIUTTO AND CHICKEN WITH PEAS IN CREAM

Ingredients

4 skinless, boneless chicken breasts

Salt and freshly ground pepper

8 sage leaves, plus additional leaves to garnish

4 large paper-thin slices prosciutto

12 oz / 350 g snow peas (mangetout)

Heaped 1 cup / 150 g frozen peas

1 scallion (spring onion), chopped

1 tbsp olive oil

½ cup / 125 ml meat, poultry or vegetable broth (stock)

¼ cup / 50 ml light (single) cream

2 tbsp lemon juice

Method

Prep and cook time: 30 min

1. Season the chicken breasts with salt and pepper and place 2 sage leaves on each one. Wrap a slice of prosciutto around each breast and secure with toothpicks (cocktail sticks).

2. Bring a saucepan of salted water to a boil and cook the snow peas (mangetout) and peas for a few minutes. Place in a colander under cold running water to stop the cooking; set aside.

3. Heat the oil in a skillet over medium heat; add the chicken and cook until browned on both sides and cooked in the center, about 10 minutes. Transfer to a plate and keep warm.

4. Return the skillet to the heat and stir in the broth (stock) and cream. Add the peas, snow peas and scallions (spring onions) and heat through. Add the lemon juice and season with salt and pepper.

5. Thickly slice the chicken breasts and serve with the peas and cream sauce. Garnish with sage leaves.

CARIBBEAN COCONUT CHICKEN

Ingredients

4 boneless chicken breasts, skinned

2 tbsp sunflower oil

1 onion, finely chopped

1 garlic clove, finely chopped

1 red bell pepper, finely chopped

1 green bell pepper, finely chopped

Generous ½ cup / 60 g grated coconut

Grated zest and juice of 1 lime

½ tsp paprika

½ tsp red chili paste

1 tsp salt

1 tbsp / 15 g butter

1 tsp apricot jam

Method

Prep and cook time: 1 hour

1. Preheat the oven to 375°F (190°C / Gas Mark 5). Put the chicken breasts between 2 sheets of plastic wrap (cling film) and, using a mallet or wooden rolling pin, beat the meat until flattened.

2. Heat the oil in a skillet (frying pan) and fry the onion and garlic over a medium heat for 2–3 minutes. Add the peppers and fry until softened. Stir in the coconut and remove the pan from the heat. Stir in the lime zest.

3. Place an equal amount of the vegetables in the center of each chicken breast. Fold the ends over the top of the filling and secure with toothpicks (cocktail sticks).

4. Put the paprika, chili paste and salt in a small bowl and mix together. Brush each chicken roll with the paste.

5. Melt the butter in a roasting pan, add the chicken rolls and bake in the oven for 25–30 minutes until golden brown, basting from time to time.

6. Remove the chicken from the pan and keep warm. Stir the apricot jam and lime juice into the pan juices. Bring to a boil, reduce the heat, and simmer for 2–3 minutes, stirring all the time. Serve the chicken with the sauce poured over the top.

CHICKEN ON A BED OF VEGETABLES

Ingredients

2 limes

1–2 tsp Chinese five-spice powder

12–14 tbsp dark soy sauce

4 chicken breast fillets

11 oz / 300 g snow peas (mangetout), trimmed

1 medium sized zucchini (courgette), sliced

7 oz / 200 g carrots, peeled and cut into matchsticks

2 tbsp oil

½ tsp chili powder

Salt

Scant ½ cup / 100 ml vegetable broth (stock)

3–4 oz / 75–100 g pea sprouts (or bean sprouts if unavailable)

2 tbsp sesame seeds (toasted)

Method

Prep and cook time: 40 min

1. Wash the lime, remove the zest with a zester and chop finely and squeeze the lime. Mix the five-spice powder, the zest and juice of the limes, and 6–8 tbsps. of the soy sauce to make a marinade; marinate the chicken for about 15 minutes.

2. Broil (grill) the chicken under a medium heat until cooked through, for 3–5 minutes on each side (depending on thickness).

3. Meanwhile, heat the oil in a wok. Add the snow peas (mangetout) and stir-fry for 1 minute. Add the zucchini (courgettes) and carrots and cook for a further 2 minutes. Sprinkle over the chili powder, 2 tbsp soy sauce, and salt. Then add the broth (stock) and cook for a further 5 minutes.

4. Wash and drain the pea sprouts and add to the vegetables with the sesame seeds. Stir-fry for a further 2 minutes.

5. Slice the chicken and drizzle with the remaining soy sauce (or to taste). Serve the stir-fried vegetables onto plates and put the chicken on top.

JERK CHICKEN

Ingredients

For the marinade:

1 onion, roughly chopped

Thumb-size piece fresh ginger, peeled and chopped

2–3 green chili peppers, halved and deseeded

1 tsp dried thyme

½ tsp grated nutmeg

1 pinch ground cinnamon

1 good pinch allspice

½ tsp ground cloves

2 tbsp sunflower oil

2 tbsp freshly squeezed lime juice

For the rest of the dish:

4 chicken legs

1 small pineapple, cut into large wedges

2 limes, halved

Thyme, to garnish

Method

Prep and cook time: 1 hour plus 2 hours to marinade

1. Put all the marinade ingredients into a liquidiser and purée finely. Score the chicken legs several times with a sharp knife and mix with the marinade. Marinate for at least 2 hours.

2. Preheat the oven to 400ºF (200ºC / Gas Mark 6) or heat the barbecue.

3. Take the chicken out of the marinade, place skin side up in a roasting pan and cook in the preheated oven for 40 minutes, or cook on the barbecue for about 15 minutes until the chicken is thoroughly cooked.

4. Meanwhile, cook the pineapple and lime halves on the barbecue, or on a heated griddle pan.

5. Serve the chicken on a bed of rice with the grilled fruit and thyme sprig to garnish.

BLACKENED INDIAN CHICKEN STICKS ON A BED OF SALAD

Ingredients

For the marinade:

3 tbsp cumin seeds

2 garlic cloves, crushed

Thumb-size piece fresh ginger, peeled and grated

4 tbsp vegetable oil

1 tsp salt

2 tsp garam masala

Juice of half a lemon

½ cup / 125 ml cup yogurt

½ tsp chili powder

4 chicken breasts, skinned

2 tbsp butter

To serve:

Arugula (rocket), cherry tomatoes and pitta breads

Method

Prep and cook time: 30 min plus 2 hours to marinate

1. Toast the cumin seeds in a dry pan for 2 minutes then crush.

2. Mix the cumin seeds with the garlic, ginger, 2 tbsp of the oil, salt, garam masala, lemon juice, yogurt and chili powder.

3. Put the chicken breasts between two sheets of plastic wrap (clingfilm) and bash with a rolling pan to flatten. Slice into strips, mix the chicken with the marinade and set aside for 2 hours.

4. Heat the butter and the remaining oil in a skillet and fry the chicken strips on all sides, basting with the marinade, until browned and cooked through.

5. Serve with the arugula (rocket), cherry tomatoes and pitta breads.

GRILLED CHICKEN WITH SWEET POTATO

Ingredients

For the marinade:

3 tbsp vegetable oil

2 tbsp honey

2 tbsp orange juice

1 clove garlic, crushed

1 red chili pepper, deseeded
and finely chopped

1 tbsp cumin seeds

Pinch saffron threads

For the rest of the dish:

4 chicken breasts, skinned

3 tbsp olive oil

1 red onion, cut into thin wedges

1 medium sweet potato, peeled
and cubed

Salt and pepper

1 cup / 150 g string beans, trimmed

Cilantro (coriander) leaves, to garnish

Method

Prep and cook time: 35 min plus
2 hours marinading time

1. Mix together all the ingredients for the
marinade and place in a shallow dish.
Add the chicken breasts and set aside to
marinade for 2 hours.

2. Heat the olive oil in a wide pan and
gently cook the onion wedges and sweet
potato until they start to soften.

3. Remove the chicken from the marinade
and add the marinade to the onion and
sweet potato. Cook gently, stirring from time
to time, then season with salt and pepper.

4. Cook the string beans in a steamer until
al dente.

5. Meanwhile, heat the broiler (grill) or
a griddle pan and cook the chicken for
5 minutes on each side or until cooked
through.

6. Break the chicken into large pieces and
add to the onion and sweet potato. Stir in
the beans and serve garnished with cilantro
(coriander).

CHICKEN BREASTS ON A BED OF VEGETABLES

Ingredients

1 lb / 450 g asparagus

1 lb / 450 g string (runner) beans

12 oz / 350 g snow (sugar snap) peas

4 boneless chicken breasts, skinned

Salt and pepper

5 tbsp / 75 g butter

4 tbsp lemon juice

4 tbsp small capers

Grated lemon zest, to garnish

Method

Prep and cook time: 40 min

1. Peel the bottom third from the asparagus stalks and trim the ends. Top and tail the beans.

2. Put the asparagus and beans in a saucepan of boiling salted water and simmer for about 6 minutes.

3. Add the snow (sugar snap) peas to the pan and continue simmering for a further 4 minutes. Drain well, immerse the vegetables in cold water and drain again. Return to the pan.

4. Season the chicken breasts with salt and pepper. Heat 2 tbsp (25 g) of butter in a skillet (frying pan) until melted. Add the chicken breasts and fry for about 5 minutes on each side until cooked through.

5. Add the remaining butter to the vegetables and heat until melted and the vegetables are hot. Add the lemon juice and season with the salt and pepper.

6. To serve, divide the vegetables and butter sauce between 4 serving plates. Put a chicken breast on top of each and sprinkle with the capers and lemon zest to garnish.

CHICKEN WITH RICOTTA STUFFING

Ingredients

1 lb 12 oz / 800 g small new potatoes

4 garlic cloves, finely chopped

½ cup / 125 ml olive oil

5 oz / 150 g ricotta cheese

Salt and pepper

4 boneless chicken thighs,
with skin on

1 lb / 450 g string (runner) beans

3 scallions (spring onions), finely
chopped

4 tbsp / 50 g butter

4 tbsp chopped fresh parsley

Method

Prep and cook time: 1 hour 20 min

1. Preheat the oven to 375°F (190°C / Gas Mark 5). Cook the potatoes in a saucepan of boiling salted water for 20–25 minutes until tender. Drain well.

2. Meanwhile, put the garlic, 2 tbsp oil and the ricotta cheese in a bowl. Season with salt and pepper and mix together.

3. Loosen the skin on the chicken thighs by running your fingers between the skin and the meat. Spoon the ricotta mixture under the skin, dividing it equally among the thighs. Season with salt and pepper.

4. Heat 2 tbsp of the oil in a roasting pan. Add the chicken thighs and sear on all sides. Roast in the oven for about 30 minutes, basting from time to time.

5. Cut the potatoes into wedges and place in a lightly greased casserole dish. Brush with the remaining oil and sprinkle with pepper. Bake in the oven for 10 minutes until you can pierce the potatoes easily with a fork.

6. Meanwhile, cook the beans in salted boiling water for about 10 minutes until tender. Drain.

7. Melt the butter in a saucepan, add the scallions and fry for 4–5 minutes. Stir in the chopped parsley. Season with salt and pepper.

8. Arrange the potatoes, beans and chicken thighs on the serving plates and serve with the scallions spooned over the top.

CHICKEN BREAST STUFFED WITH TOMATO

Ingredients

4 oz / 120 g dried tomatoes in oil

4 tbsp chopped fresh basil

3 tbsp grated Parmesan cheese

1 tbsp toasted pine nuts

3 tbsp olive oil

Salt and pepper

2 large red bell peppers

1 tbsp vegetable oil, for greasing

4 boneless chicken breasts, skinned

1 tbsp lemon juice

8 slices bacon

Method

Prep and cook time: 50 min

1. Preheat the oven to 375°F (190°C / Gas Mark 5). Drain the tomatoes and finely chop.

2. To make the pesto, put the basil, Parmesan cheese, pine nuts and olive oil in a food processor and blend together to form a purée. Season with salt and pepper.

3. Remove the stems, cores and seeds from the peppers and cut into quarters. Place, skin side up, in a lightly greased ovenproof dish. Brush a little oil on the peppers.

4. Make a horizontal cut along each chicken breast to form a pocket. Rub each breast, inside and out, with the lemon juice, salt and pepper. Fill the pockets with the tomatoes and pesto.

5. Wrap each chicken breast with two strips of bacon and put in the prepared dish with the peppers.

6. Bake in the oven for about 25 minutes, until tender and cooked through.

CHICKEN PARMIGIANA

Ingredients

1 garlic clove, chopped

14 oz / 400 g can chopped tomatoes

1 tsp dried basil

1 tsp dried thyme

½ tsp sugar

Salt and pepper

8 thin chicken escalopes

2 eggs

¾ cup / 75 g grated Parmesan cheese

1½ cups / 85 g breadcrumbs

Vegetable oil, for shallow frying

7 oz / 200 g mozzarella cheese

Fresh basil, to garnish

Method

Prep and cook time: 50 min

1. To make the sauce, put the garlic in a small saucepan with the tomatoes, dried basil, thyme and sugar. Bring to the boil then simmer for about 15 minutes, stirring occasionally.

2. Using a hand-held blender, blend the ingredients together to form a smooth purée. Season to taste with salt and pepper. Set aside.

3. Put the chicken escalopes between two sheets of plastic wrap (cling film) and beat with a meat mallet or rolling pin to flatten.

4. Separate the eggs into 2 large bowls. Whisk the egg whites in a large bowl until stiff and then fold into the egg yolks with ½ cup / 50 g of the Parmesan cheese.

5. Spread the breadcrumbs on to a large plate. Dip the escalopes into the egg mixture and then into the breadcrumbs, coating both sides.

6. Meanwhile, preheat the broiler (grill). Heat the oil in a large skillet (frying pan) and fry the escalopes on both sides for about 3 minutes.

7. Place the escalopes on a heatproof dish, overlapping slightly in pairs. Slice the mozzarella cheese and lay on top of the escalopes. Put under the broiler for about 5 minutes.

8. Put 2 escalopes on each plate and spoon over the sauce. Sprinkle with the remaining Parmesan cheese and serve immediately with spaghetti and garnished with fresh basil.

CHICKEN AU GRATIN WITH CHERRY TOMATOES

Ingredients

4 chicken breasts, skinned

2 balls mozzarella, approx. 8 oz / 225 g each, sliced

4 tsp pesto

1 tbsp fresh sage, chopped

5 slices stale white bread, crusts removed, grated

Olive oil

Salt and pepper

1 garlic clove, finely chopped

1 lb / 450 g cherry tomatoes, halved

2/3 cup / 150 ml dry white wine

Method

Prep and cook time: 50 min

1. Heat the oven to 350°F (180°C / Gas Mark 4).

2. Cut a pocket in the side of each chicken breast. Place the mozzarella slices and a teaspoon of pesto in each pockets and close with a toothpick (cocktail stick).

3. Mix together the sage and breadcrumbs with a little oil until a thick paste is formed. Season with salt and ground black pepper.

4. Place the garlic and the tomatoes in a baking dish, pour the white wine over the top and add oil. Season with salt and pepper. Place the chicken on top and spread with the breadcrumb mixture. Bake for about 30 minutes until golden brown and the chicken is thoroughly cooked. Serve immediately.

CHICKEN SALTIMBOCCA

Ingredients

3 tbsp olive oil, plus extra to grease

4 boneless chicken breasts, skinned

7 oz / 200 g mozzarella cheese

8 slices prosciutto

8 sage leaves

Salt and pepper

7 tbsp dry white wine

Small bunch watercress, to garnish

Method

Prep and cook time: 35 min

1. Preheat the oven to 400°F (200°C / Gas Mark 6). Lightly oil a roasting pan.

2. Slice each chicken breast in half horizontally. Beat with a meat mallet or wooden rolling pin to flatten slightly.

3. Heat 2 tbsp oil in a large skillet (frying pan) and briefly brown the chicken pieces on both sides. Remove from the pan and place in the prepared roasting pan.

4. Slice the mozzarella cheese. Put a prosciutto slice, a sage leaf and 2 slices of mozzarella cheese on each chicken breast. Season lightly with salt and pepper.

5. Cook in the oven for about 8 minutes until golden brown.

6. Remove the chicken pieces from the roasting pan once they are cooked through. Add the wine to the pan and heat, stirring all the time to deglaze the pan, until the sauce has reduced slightly.

7. Serve the saltimbocca with the sauce poured over the top and garnish with the watercress.

CHICKEN BREASTS IN COCONUT MILK

Ingredients

1 carrot, roughly chopped

1 leek, roughly chopped

2 celery stalks, roughly chopped

1 bay leaf

2 boneless chicken breasts, with skin on

1 tbsp / 15 g butter

1 tbsp sugar

1 red chili, deseeded and finely chopped

2 tsp finely chopped fresh ginger

1 cup / 225 ml coconut milk

Salt and pepper

6 oz / 150 g corn salad (lamb's lettuce)

3 tbsp olive oil

2 tbsp balsamic vinegar

1 cup / 35 g basil leaves, chopped

Method

Prep and cook time: 45 min

1. Lay the chicken breasts on top of the vegetables, add enough water just to cover the meat and bring to a gentle boil. Simmer for about 15 minutes and remove from the heat.

2. Melt the butter and sugar in a clean pan over high heat and allow to caramelize slightly. As soon as the sugar starts to caramelize add the chopped chili and ginger. Pour in the coconut milk and cook until reduced slightly. Season with salt and pepper.

3. Arrange the corn salad (lamb's lettuce) on a serving dish. Dress with the olive oil and balsamic vinegar.

4. Add the basil leaves to the coconut milk sauce.

5. Remove the chicken breasts from the pan and slice. Add to the serving plates and drizzle over the sauce to serve.

PIRI PIRI CHICKEN

Ingredients

4 fresh red chilies

½ cup / 100 ml olive oil

2 garlic cloves

1 tsp dried oregano

2 tsp paprika

¼ cup / 50 ml red wine vinegar

Salt and pepper

4 boneless chicken breasts, with skin on

1 red bell pepper

1 yellow bell pepper

1 tbsp chopped fresh parsley, to garnish

Method

Prep and cook time: 1 hour plus 1 hour marinating

1. Preheat the oven to 375°F (190°C / Gas Mark 5). Put the chilies in a roasting pan with a little of the oil and roast in the oven for 10 minutes. Leave to cool. Meanwhile, finely chop the garlic.

2. Roughly chop the cooled chilies, discarding the seeds. Put the chilies, garlic, oregano, paprika, olive oil and vinegar in a saucepan, and simmer for 2–3 minutes. Season with salt.

3. Using a hand-held blender or mini food processor, blend the mixture to form a purée.

4. Put the chicken, in a single layer, in a shallow dish and spread half the piri piri sauce evenly over the chicken. Cover and leave to marinate for 1 hour.

5. Increase the oven temperature to 400°F (200°C / Gas Mark 6). Preheat a large ridged skillet or griddle pan. Season the marinated

chicken with pepper and cook, skin side down, on the pan for 2–3 minutes until golden brown. Turn and cook for a further 2 minutes.

6. Transfer the griddled chicken to a roasting pan and roast in the oven for 30 minutes or until cooked through, basting regularly with the remaining piri piri sauce.

7. Meanwhile, cut the red and yellow peppers into chunky pieces, discarding the cores and seeds. Thread the pieces on to 4 bamboo skewers and griddle for 10 minutes.

8. To serve, slice the chicken and accompany with the griddled peppers and tomato salsa and boiled rice, if wished. Sprinkle over chopped parsley to garnish.

COQ AU VIN

Ingredients

4 tbsp all-purpose (plain) flour

Salt and pepper

1 chicken, cut into 4 pieces

10 tbsp / 150 g butter

8 oz / 225 g shallots

1 garlic clove, crushed

4 oz / 120 g thickly sliced bacon, diced

8 oz / 225 g chestnut mushrooms

1 bottle dry white wine

3 sprigs fresh thyme plus some for garnish

For the beurre manié

2 tbsp / 25 g butter

¼ cup / 25 g all-purpose (plain) flour

Method

Prep and cook time: 1 hour

1. Preheat the oven to 350°F (180°C / Gas Mark 4).

2. Put the flour into a large shallow dish and season generously with salt and pepper. Dip the chicken portions in the flour to coat.

3. Melt the butter in a large flameproof casserole dish. When foaming, add the chicken portions and fry until browned all over, turning as needed.

4. Add the shallots, garlic and diced bacon and fry until golden brown. Stir in the mushrooms. Pour in the wine and add the thyme. Bring to the boil then cover the casserole.

5. Cook in the oven for 40 minutes until the chicken and vegetables are tender.

6. Put the butter and flour for the beurre manié in a small bowl and mix together. Return the coq au vin to the heat and cook over a medium heat, stirring in the beurre manié, a small piece at a time, until the sauce thickens slightly and is glossy. Serve garnished with fresh thyme.

CHICKEN WITH PEPPER SAUCE

Ingredients

2 tbsp olive oil

2 onions, chopped

1 garlic clove, chopped

3 red bell peppers, sliced

$2/3$ cup / 150 ml vegetable broth (stock)

Salt and pepper

4 boneless chicken breasts, skinned

1 tbsp / 15 g butter

1 tbsp olive oil

1 lb / 450 g green tagliatelle

4 tbsp pitted (stoned) black olives, sliced

Method

Prep and cook time: 45 min

1. Heat the oil in a large saucepan, add the onion and fry until translucent. Add the garlic and the red peppers. Fry for a further 3 minutes.

2. Pour in the vegetable broth (stock). Cover the pan and simmer for about 10 minutes. Using a hand-held blender, purée the sauce.

3. Return to the pan and simmer, uncovered, for about 5 minutes. Season to taste with salt and pepper.

4. Meanwhile, cut the chicken into thick slices and season with salt and pepper.

5. Heat the butter and olive oil in a large skillet (frying pan). Add the chicken pieces and fry for 3–4 minutes on each side until cooked through. Sprinkle generously with pepper.

6. Cook the tagliatelle according to the packet instructions until tender but still with a slight bite.

7. Drain the tagliatelle and divide between 4 plates. Add the chicken with the sauce and serve sprinkled with the sliced olives, to garnish.

PERSIAN CHICKEN

Ingredients

1 cup / 200 g yellow split lentils

4 cups / 1 liter water

1 tsp salt

2 tbsp / 25 g butter

4 boneless chicken breasts, skinned and chopped into bite-size pieces

1 large onion, chopped

2 garlic cloves, crushed

2 tsp garam masala

1 tsp curcuma (turmeric)

1 tsp hot chili powder

1 cup / 200 g canned chopped tomatoes

Fresh spinach leaves, to garnish

Method
Prep and cook time: 1 hour 15 min

1. Put the lentils in a saucepan with the water and salt. Bring to the boil, then cover and simmer for 30 minutes until the lentils are tender and have absorbed most of the water.

2. Melt the butter in a large skillet (frying pan) or flameproof casserole. Add the chicken and fry for 5 minutes until golden on all sides.

3. Add the onion, garlic, garam masala, curcuma (turmeric) and chili powder and gently fry for 5 minutes until the onion is softened.

4. Add the tomatoes, cooked lentils and 4 tbsp of water. Cover and simmer gently for 30 minutes until the chicken is tender and cooked through. Serve with noodles or rice, if wished, and garnish with fresh spinach leaves.

CREAMY CHICKEN WITH LEEKS

Ingredients

2 tbsp olive oil

1 onion, chopped

4 baby leeks, shredded

4 boneless chicken breasts, skinned and cut into thick slices

Salt and pepper

1 tbsp all-purpose (plain) flour

1¼ cups / 300 ml chicken broth (stock)

¾ cup / 200 ml crème fraîche

2 tbsp chopped fresh tarragon

Lime wedges, to garnish

Method

Prep and cook time: 40 min

1. Heat the oil in a large skillet (frying pan) and add the onion and leeks. Cook gently for 2 minutes, then remove 1 tbsp of the lightly cooked leeks and set aside to garnish.

2. Add the chicken to the pan, season generously with salt and pepper and cook for 5 minutes until browned on all sides.

3. Sprinkle over the flour and cook for 1 minute, then gradually stir in the broth (stock). Cover the pan and simmer for 15 minutes.

4. Stir the crème fraîche and tarragon into the chicken and heat through for 2–3 minutes. Check that the chicken is thoroughly cooked through. Serve the chicken with rice and garnish with the reserved leeks and a lime wedge.

CHICKEN CACCIATORE

Ingredients

1 tbsp olive oil

1 onion, finely chopped

1 garlic clove, crushed

1 tsp chopped fresh oregano, plus extra to garnish

1 lb 8 oz / 650 g boneless chicken thighs, skinned and cut into chunks

½ tsp celery salt

Salt and pepper

7 tbsp / 100 ml white wine

14 oz / 400 g can chopped tomatoes

½ tsp sugar

Black olives, to garnish

Method
Prep and cook time: 50 min

1. Heat the oil in a skillet (frying pan), add the onions, garlic and oregano and fry for about 3 minutes, until softened.

2. Add the chicken pieces, sprinkle in the celery salt and season with pepper. Cook for 10 minutes, turning occasionally, until lightly browned.

3. Pour in the wine and bring to a simmer. Add the tomatoes and sugar, cover with a lid and leave to simmer for 20 minutes until the chicken is tender and cooked through.

4. Serve the chicken garnished with black olives and oregano and accompany with the pasta.

CHICKEN AND PEPPER FRICASSÉE

Ingredients

2 tbsp olive oil

2 skinless boneless chicken breasts, cut into small pieces

1 onion, chopped

2 carrots, trimmed and chopped

1 red bell pepper, sliced

2½ cups / 600 ml chicken broth (stock)

1 cup / 200 g sweet corn kernels, optional

1 chopped scallion (spring onion), to garnish

Method

Prep and cook time: 1 hour

1. Heat the oven to 375 F (190C / Gas Mark 5).

2. Heat the oil in a large flameproof casserole, add the chicken and fry for a few minutes to brown. Add the onion and carrots and cook, stirring, for a few minutes to soften. Stir in the red bell pepper and cook for 2 more minutes.

3. Pour in the broth (stock) and corn and bring to a boil. Cover and carefully transfer to the oven. Bake for 50 minutes until the chicken and vegetables are tender.

5. Serve the chicken fricassée with couscous and garnish with chopped scallion (spring onion).

CHICKEN WITH MUSHROOMS AND LEEKS

Ingredients

4 chicken breasts, skinned

3 tbsp / 45 g butter

2 tbsp vegetable oil

8 oz / 250 g button mushrooms, thinly sliced

1 leek, sliced

½ cup / 125 ml light (single) cream

2 tbsp chopped parsley, to garnish

Method

Prep and cook time: 45 min

1. Season the chicken breasts with salt and pepper. Heat 1 tbsp butter with 1 tbsp oil in a wide skillet and gently cook the chicken breasts for about 4 minutes each side or until golden brown and cooked through. Set aside and keep warm.

2. Heat the remaining butter and oil in the skillet, scraping up any meat residue with a wooden spoon and add the mushrooms. Cook for 3 minutes over a medium high heat then stir in the leeks and reduce the heat.

3. Cook gently until the leeks are soft but not brown then pour over the cream, let bubble and season with salt and pepper.

4. Put the chicken on warmed serving plates, pour over the sauce, garnish with parsley and serve immediately with mashed potatoes.

CHICKEN AND PEPPER FAJITAS FILLING

Ingredients

6 tbsp olive oil

Juice of 1 lime

1 tsp sweet paprika

Salt and pepper

2 chicken breasts, skinned

1 onion, finely sliced

1 clove garlic, finely chopped

1 red bell pepper, deseeded and sliced

1 yellow bell pepper, deseeded and sliced

1 green bell pepper, deseeded and sliced

1 red chili pepper, deseeded and finely chopped

½ cup / 125 ml chicken broth (stock)

1 lime, cut into wedges to garnish

Parsley sprigs, to serve

Fajitas, to serve

Method

Prep and cook time: 25 min plus
30 min to marinate

1. Mix 2 tbsp of the olive oil with the lime juice and paprika, season with salt and pepper and rub into the chicken breasts. Set aside to marinade for 30 minutes.

2. Heat 3 tbsp oil in a deep skillet and gently cook the onion until softened but not brown. Add the garlic, bell peppers and chili pepper and cook for 5 minutes.

3. Pour over the chicken broth (stock), season with salt and pepper and let bubble until most of the liquid has evaporated. Set aside and keep warm.

4. Brush a clean skillet or griddle pan with the remaining oil and heat until smoking. Cook the chicken breasts for about 4 minutes each side or until cooked through and golden brown.

5. Slice the chicken and arrange on the peppers. Garnish with lime wedges and parsley and serve with fajitas.

CHICKEN CAPONATA

Ingredients

4 chicken legs

8 sage leaves

2 garlic cloves, chopped

2 red chili peppers, deseeded and chopped

4 tbsp olive oil

2 tbsp lemon juice

For the caponata:

4 tomatoes

2 tbsp olive oil

1 medium eggplant (aubergine), coarsely chopped

1 yellow bell pepper, sliced

1 onion, sliced

1 celery stalk, sliced (leaves reserved for garnish)

½ cup / 50 g pitted black olives

1 tbsp capers

White wine vinegar

Salt and freshly ground pepper

Method

Prep and cook time: 1 hour 10 min

1. Preheat the oven to 350F (180C / Gas Mark 4).

2. Take the chicken legs and separate the drumstick from the thigh at the joint. Put one sage leaf under the skin of each piece of chicken.

3. Mix together the garlic, chili pepper, olive oil and lemon juice. Rub into the chicken and put in a roasting pan.

4. Bake the chicken in the preheated oven for about 40 minutes until golden brown.

5. Blanch the tomatoes, immerse in cold water and remove the skins. Slice into quarters and remove the seeds.

6. Sauté the eggplant (aubergine) in hot oil until lightly browned.

7. Add the bell pepper, onion and sliced celery. Season with salt and pepper. Cook, covered, for about 10 minutes, stirring occasionally.

8. Add the tomatoes, olives and capers. Cook, uncovered, for about 4 minutes more. Season to taste with the vinegar, salt and pepper.

9 Divide the vegetables among the plates and arrange the chicken pieces on top. Garnish with the reserved celery leaves and serve.

CHICKEN AND VEGETABLE STIR-FRY

Ingredients

5–6 tbsp vegetable oil, divided

1 lb / 500 g skinless boneless chicken breast, sliced into thin strips

Salt and freshly ground pepper

2 large red bell peppers, sliced into strips

2 cloves garlic, minced

2 young thin leeks, thinly sliced (white and light green parts only)

2 tsp minced fresh ginger root

1 tsp instant chicken or beef bouillon granules

5–6 tbsp soy sauce

1 cup / about 100 g bean sprouts

2 tbsp chopped cilantro (coriander) leaves

Method

Prep and cook time: 25 min

1. Heat 2 tablespoons of oil in a wok or large skillet over high heat; stir-fry the chicken until cooked through, about 2–4 minutes. Season with salt and pepper; transfer to a plate and keep warm.

2. Return the wok to the heat, add the rest of the oil, and stir-fry the bell peppers and garlic for 2–3 minutes. Add the leeks, ginger, 5–6 tablespoons water and the broth granules; cover and cook for a further 3 minutes. Stir in the soy sauce and season with salt and pepper.

3. Return the chicken to the wok, add the bean sprouts and heat through. Sprinkle with cilantro (coriander) and serve with rice.

CHICKEN WITH ORANGE ZEST

Ingredients

2 oranges

2 garlic cloves, chopped

4 skinless boneless chicken breasts, cut into bite-size cubes

1 lb / 450 g glass (bean thread, cellophane) noodles

1 tbsp cornstarch (cornflour)

3 tbsp sesame oil

1 tbsp honey

Light soy sauce, to taste

Cayenne pepper, to taste

1 scallion (spring onion), green parts only, very thinly sliced on the diagonal, to garnish

Method

Prep and cook time: 30 min plus 8 hours to marinate

1. Finely grate the zest of one orange and remove the zest of the other in fine strips. Juice both oranges.

2. In a medium bowl, mix together the grated orange zest, orange juice and garlic. Add the chicken and toss to coat. Cover and marinate in the refrigerator for at least 8 hours or overnight.

3. Cook the noodles according to the instructions on the package; rinse in a colander under cold running water, drain and set aside.

4. Remove the chicken from the marinade and drain well, reserving the marinade. Spread the cornstarch (cornflour) on a plate and toss with the chicken to coat the chicken.

5. Heat the oil in a wok or skillet until smoking, then add the chicken and cook, stirring, until browned all over. Add the honey and heat through. Pour in the reserved marinade and cook, stirring to loosen browned bits from the bottom of the skillet. Simmer, stirring frequently, for about 3–4 minutes or until the chicken is cooked.

6. Season with soy sauce and cayenne pepper and add the orange zest strips.

7. Place the drained noodles on plates or a large platter. Arrange the orange chicken on top and sprinkle with the scallion rings.

KUNG PAO

Ingredients

3 tbsp vegetable oil

4 skinless boneless chicken breasts, cut into cubes

3 red chili peppers, seeded and sliced into thin strips

3 garlic cloves, roughly chopped

2 scallions (spring onions), finely chopped

½ cup / 75 g peanuts

1 tsp sugar

2 tbsp rice wine

Soy sauce, to taste

Method

Prep and cook time: 20 min

1. In a large skillet or wok, heat the vegetable oil until very hot. Add the chicken and chilies and stir-fry until the chicken is seared, 2–3 minutes.

2. Add the garlic, scallions (spring onions), peanuts and sugar and continue frying for 1–2 minutes.

3. Add the rice wine and a little water, if needed, and simmer for 1–2 minutes, until cooked. Season with soy sauce and serve at once.

CHICKEN JALFREZI

Ingredients

1 lb 2 oz / 500 g chicken breast fillets, sliced into thin strips

1 tbsp Worcestershire sauce

3 tbsp oil

A good pinch of brown mustard seeds

A good pinch of cumin seeds

3 onions, sliced

2 red chilies, or more according to taste, deseeded and finely chopped

A good pinch of ground cumin

A pinch of ground coriander

A good pinch of ground curcuma (turmeric)

7 oz / 200 g sugarsnap peas, trimmed

1 cup / 150 g frozen peas, thawed

$^2/_3$ – ¾ cup / 150–200 ml coconut cream, to taste

Salt & freshly milled pepper

Mint leaves

Method
Prep and cook time: 25 min

1. Mix the chicken with the Worcestershire sauce.

2. Heat the oil in a skillet and fry the mustard seeds and cumin seeds, stirring, for about 30 seconds, until they start to pop. Add the onions and chilies and fry, stirring, until the onions are lightly browned.

3. Stir in the meat, ground spices, Worcestershire sauce, sugarsnap peas and thawed frozen peas and season with salt and pepper. Add 1 cup of water, bring to a boil and cook over a medium heat for a further 3–5 minutes, stirring, until the meat and vegetables are just cooked.

4. Add coconut cream to taste. Sprinkle with mint and serve with rice.

COCONUT CHICKEN

Ingredients

3 tbsp sesame oil

1 onion, finely diced

2 cloves garlic, finely diced

1 red chili, deseeded and shredded

½ lime, zest and juice

2 tsp freshly grated ginger

3¼ cups / 800 ml coconut milk

1⅓ cup / 200 g frozen peas

1 lb 2 oz / 500 g chicken breast, cut into strips

Salt

Brown sugar

Soy sauce

Cilantro (coriander) leaves, to garnish

Method

Prep and cook time: 30 min

1. Heat 2 tablespoons sesame oil in a wok or a large skillet. Add the garlic, diced onion, grated ginger, chili and lime zest and sauté briefly. Pour in the coconut milk and cook for about 10 minutes over a low heat until reduced slightly. Add the frozen peas after about 5 minutes.

2. At the end of the 10 minutes add the chicken and cook very gently in the sauce for a few minutes until the meat is done. Add salt, sugar, lime juice and soy sauce to taste.

3. Serve the chicken with rice and garnish with cilantro (coriander).

CHICKEN WITH OYSTER SAUCE AND NOODLES

Ingredients

1½ lb / 600 g skinless boneless chicken breasts, chopped into bite-size pieces

Salt and freshly ground pepper

5 tbsp sesame oil, divided

4-inch / 10-cm piece lemongrass

1 lb / 400 g udon noodles

1 garlic clove, minced

1 scallion (spring onion), finely chopped

3 tbsp oyster sauce

2 tbsp light soy sauce

1 tsp sugar

Method

Prep and cook time: 20 min plus 30 min to marinate

1. In a small bowl, mix the chicken with salt, pepper, lemongrass and 2 tbsp of the sesame oil; marinate for 30 minutes.

2. Cook the noodles in boiling salted water according to package instructions; drain and set aside.

3. Heat the remaining 3 tbsp of oil in a wok or large skillet and stir-fry the garlic and the scallion (spring onion) for 30 seconds. Add the chicken and fry all together for 3–4 minutes, until the chicken is cooked through. Season with oyster sauce, soy sauce and sugar; discard the lemongrass stalk.

4. Toss the noodles with the chicken and the sauce and heat through; serve at once.

SOUR CHICKEN CURRY

Ingredients

2 chicken breasts (1 lb 2 oz/500 g)

2 tbsp soy sauce

1 cup / 200 g rice

1 pinch each of curcuma (turmeric), chili powder, cinnamon

1 onion, finely diced

2 green bell peppers, deseeded and cut into thin strips

7 oz / 200 g snow peas (mangetout), cut into thin strips

1 red chili, deseeded and cut into thin strips

1 tbsp sesame oil

Scant ½ cup / 100 ml vegetable broth (stock)

Curry powder (1 good pinch of each of the following ground spices: coriander, black pepper, ginger, paprika, nutmeg, mustard seed, cloves, cardamom, fenugreek, cumin)

2 tbsp lemon juice

Salt

Method
Prep and cook time: 45 min

1. Preheat the oven to 325°F (160°C / Gas Mark 3). Cut the chicken breast into thin strips and sprinkle with soy sauce.

2. Put the rice into a pan with just double the amount of lightly salted water and bring to a boil. Cover and cook over a very low heat for about 20 minutes

3. Mix the curcuma (turmeric), chili powder and cinnamon. Sprinkle the mix over the meat and knead into it.

4. Heat the oil in a nonstick skillet (frying pan) and sauté the chicken on all sides, until it is cooked through. Take out of the skillet, put on a plate, cover with aluminum foil and keep warm in the preheated oven.

5. Put the prepared vegetables into the skillet and fry lightly. Add the vegetable broth (stock) and curry powder, to taste, and simmer for 3–5 minutes. Season with salt and pepper and add lemon juice to taste. Add the cooked rice to the vegetables and mix well.

6. Spoon into bowls. Put the chicken on top of the vegetable rice and serve hot.

PAD THAI

Ingredients

8 oz / 225 g rice noodles

2 boneless chicken breasts, skinned

2 tbsp soy sauce

2–3 tbsp oyster sauce

1 onion

3 garlic cloves

1 red chili

2 scallions (spring onions)

1 lime

5 oz / 150 g unsalted cashew nuts

3 tbsp vegetable oil

Salt and pepper

8 oz / 225 g peeled shrimp (prawns)

2/3 cup / 150 ml chicken broth (stock)

Fresh cilantro (coriander),
to garnish

Method

Prep and cook time: 45 min

1. Cook the noodles according to the packet instructions. Rinse under cold water and drain well.

2. Meanwhile, slice the chicken breasts into thin strips. Put in a large bowl, add the soy and oyster sauces and leave to marinate for a few minutes.

3. Chop the onion and finely chop the garlic. Finely slice the chili, discarding the seeds. Finely chop the white parts of the scallions (spring onions) and slice the green parts on the diagonal into rings. Cut the lime into 8 wedges. Roughly chop the cashew nuts.

4. Heat the oil in a wok. Add the chicken slices, reserving the marinade, and sear quickly. Remove from the wok and season with salt.

5. Add the onions, garlic and chili to the remaining oil in the wok. Add the shrimps (prawns) and fry briefly. Pour in the broth (stock) and simmer for 2 minutes.

6. Mix the noodles, chicken and reserved marinade together. Season with salt and pepper. Add the scallions and mix together.

7. Turn the mixture into the wok and heat until the chicken is thoroughly cooked. Serve sprinkled with the cashew nuts, garnished with cilantro (coriander) sprigs and accompanied with the lime wedges.

CHICKEN AND CASHEW STIR-FRY

Ingredients

4 tbsp sesame oil

4 chicken breasts, skinned and cut into chunks

2 tbsp cornstarch (cornflour)

1 green chili pepper, deseeded and chopped

1 green bell pepper, deseeded and chopped

3 scallions (spring onions), sliced

8 canned water chestnuts, sliced

½ cup / 75 g cashew nuts

4 tbsp oyster sauce

Juice of 1 lime

2–3 tbsp light soy sauce

Method

Prep and cook time: 25 min

1. Heat the oil in a wok or deep skillet until smoking. Dust the chicken pieces with the cornstarch and stir-fry them for 3–4 minutes or until slightly crispy. Remove the chicken from the wok.

2. Add a little more oil to the wok and fry the chili pepper for 1 minute. Add the bell pepper and scallions (spring onions) and cook for 2 more minutes.

3. Return the chicken to the wok with the water chestnuts and cashew nuts. Stir in the oyster sauce, lime juice and soy sauce and serve immediately with rice.

CHICKEN CHOW MEIN

Ingredients

For the noodles:

8 oz / 225 g dried egg noodles

1 tbsp sesame oil

For the chicken and marinade:

2 tsp light soy sauce

2 tsp rice wine or dry sherry

1 tsp sesame oil

½ tsp freshly ground white pepper

4 oz / 100 g skinless boneless chicken breast, cut into matchsticks

For the stir-fry:

3 tbsp vegetable oil, divided

1 tbsp minced garlic

½ cup / 50 g snow peas or sugar snap peas, thinly sliced lengthwise

⅓ cup / 50 g shredded cooked ham

2 tsp light soy sauce

2 tsp dark soy sauce

1 tbsp rice wine or dry sherry

1 tsp salt

½ tsp freshly ground pepper

½ tsp sugar

3 tbsp scallions (spring onions), chopped

Method
Prep and cook time: 40 min

1. Cook the noodles in a large pot of boiling water for 3–5 minutes, then drain and refresh in cold water. Toss with the sesame oil and set aside.

2. Combine the soy sauce, rice wine or sherry, sesame oil, salt and white pepper in a medium bowl; add the chicken and toss to coat. Let stand 10 minutes to marinate.

3. Heat a skillet or wok over high heat. Add 1 tbsp of the vegetable oil and when very hot and slightly smoking, add the shredded chicken. Stir-fry for about 2 minutes, then transfer to a plate.

4. Return the wok to the heat, then add the remaining 2 tablespoons vegetable oil. When slightly smoking, add the garlic and stir-fry for 10 seconds. Then add the snow peas or sugar snaps and ham and stir-fry for about 1 minute.

5. Add the chicken with its juices and the light and dark soy sauce; stir-fry for 3–4 minutes until chicken is nearly cooked. Add the rice wine or sherry, salt, pepper, sugar and scallions. Stir-fry for 2 minutes.

6. Add the noodles and sesame oil and give the mixture a few final stirs to reheat. Turn onto a warm platter and serve at once.

CHINESE-STYLE CHICKEN

Ingredients

2 red bell peppers

7 oz / 200 g can bamboo shoots

4 scallions (spring onions)

4 boneless chicken breasts, skinned

4 tbsp vegetable oil

5 tbsp soy sauce

1 tbsp cornstarch (cornflour)

Salt and pepper

$^{1}/_{3}$ cup / 50 g cashew nuts

1½ cups / 150 g bean sprouts

2 tbsp oyster sauce

Method
Prep and cook time: 25 min

1. Slice the red peppers into fine strips, discarding the cores and seeds. Roughly chop the bamboo shoots. Roughly chop the scallions (spring onions). Slice the chicken breasts into thick strips.

2. Heat the oil in a wok or large skillet (frying pan), add the chicken and stir-fry for 4 minutes. Remove from the pan and set aside.

3. Add the peppers, bamboo shoots and scallions and stir-fry for 3 minutes.

4. Mix the soy sauce with the cornstarch (cornflour) and add a little water to make a smooth paste. Stir into the vegetables.

5. Return the chicken to the pan and season with salt and pepper.

6. Stir in the cashew nuts and bean sprouts, heat briefly, check the chicken is cooked through, and season to taste with the oyster sauce. Serve in bowls.

SESAME CHICKEN WITH CASHEWS

Ingredients

1 egg white

2 tsp cornstarch (cornflour)

½ tsp salt

4 skinless boneless chicken breasts

2 tbsp vegetable oil, divided

1 tbsp black sesame seeds

2 tsp dark soy sauce

2 tsp cider vinegar

2 tsp chili bean sauce

1 tbsp sesame oil

2 tsp sugar

1 tbsp rice wine or dry sherry

4 scallions (spring onions), roughly chopped

1 red bell pepper, sliced

1 cup / 200 g baby corn, cut into bite-size pieces

4 tbsp cashew nuts

Method

Prep and cook time: 35 min

1. In a medium bowl, whisk together the egg white, cornstarch and salt. Add the chicken and stir to coat. Refrigerate for 15 minutes.

2. Meanwhile, to prepare the sauce, heat 1 tbsp of the vegetable oil in a small skillet. Add the sesame seeds and stir-fry for 30 seconds until fragrant. Stir in the soy sauce, cider vinegar, chili bean sauce, sesame oil, sugar and rice wine or dry sherry. Bring to a boil, then remove from the heat and set aside.

3. Bring 1½ cups / 350 ml of water to a boil in a large skillet or wok. Add the chicken, reduce the heat and simmer until cooked through. Drain, discarding the water. Add the cooked chicken to the sauce and warm through.

4. Return the skillet to the heat and add the remaining tablespoon vegetable oil. Add the scallions (spring onion), red bell pepper, corn and cashews and stir-fry until the vegetables are softened, 3–5 minutes.

5. Divide the vegetable mixture into 4 bowls. Cut each chicken breast into 5 slices and arrange on top of the vegetables. Drizzle with the sesame sauce and serve at once.

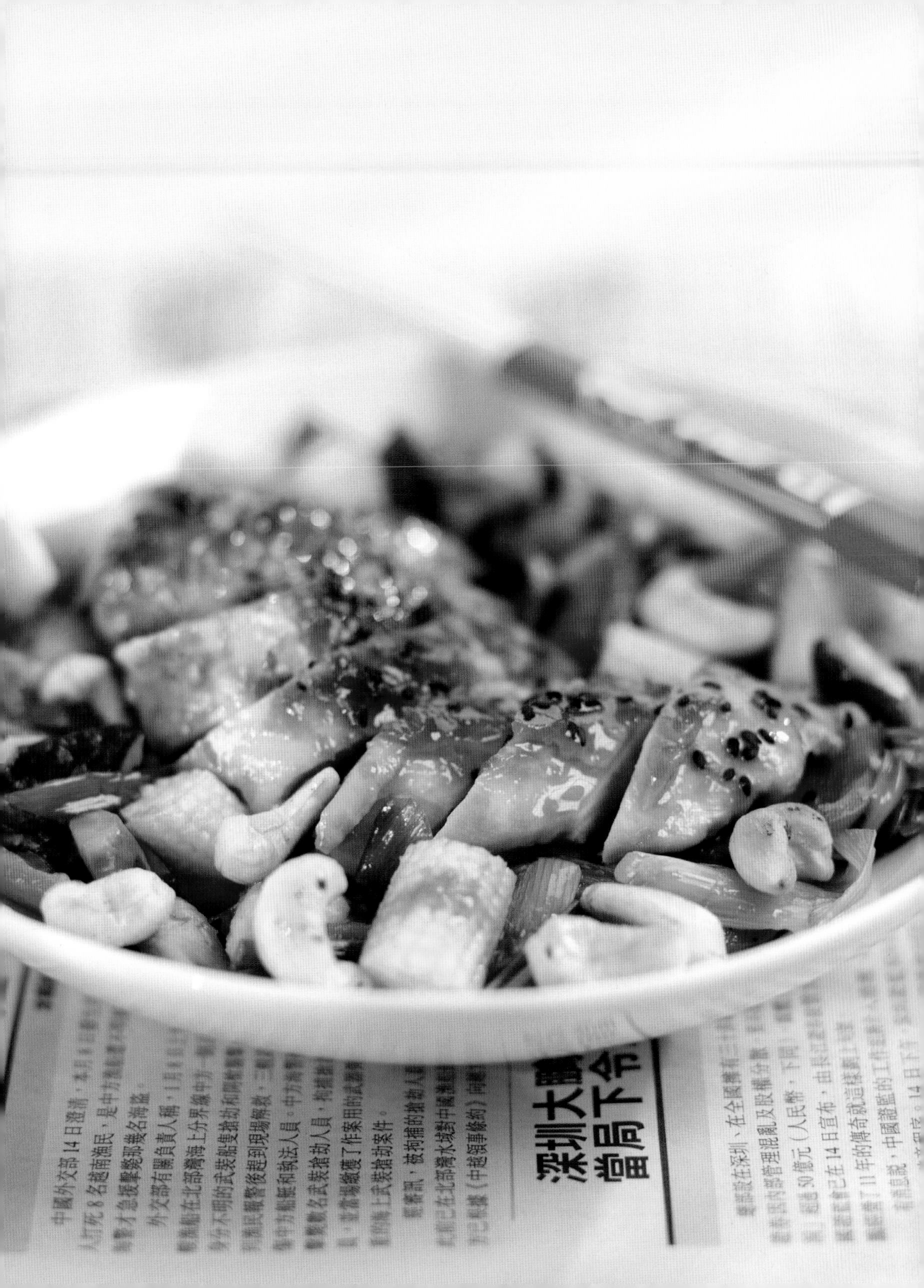

STIR-FRIED CHICKEN WITH GINGER

Ingredients

1 lb / 500 g skinless boneless chicken breasts, sliced into strips

1 egg white

1 tbsp all-purpose (plain) flour

3 tbsp vegetable oil

2 scallions (spring onions), thinly sliced

1 tsp minced fresh ginger root

1 red bell pepper, diced

1 small hot chili pepper, finely chopped

2 tbsp rice wine

1-2 tbsp soy sauce

1 tbsp black bean paste

Method

Prep and cook time: 30 min

1. Combine the chicken with the egg white in a medium bowl. Blend the flour to a smooth paste with 2 tablespoons of water and mix with the chicken.

2. Heat the oil in a large skillet or wok and sauté the chicken until firm. Transfer to a plate and keep warm; return the wok to the heat.

3. Add the scallions (spring onions) and ginger; sauté lightly. Add the bell pepper, chili pepper, wine, soy sauce and bean paste; return the chicken to the wok and stir-fry for a few minutes, until cooked through. Season to taste and serve with rice.

INDONESIAN NOODLES WITH CHICKEN AND SHRIMPS

Ingredients

12 oz / 350 g thin egg noodles

8 tbsp vegetable oil

1 lb 2 oz / 500 g boneless chicken breasts, cut into ½ inch / 1.5 cm slices

6 scallions (spring onions), chopped

2 onions, finely chopped

3 garlic cloves, crushed

6 oz / 175 g pak choi, cut into quarters

2 red chilies, finely sliced

1 tbsp finely chopped fresh ginger

8 oz / 225 g raw shrimp (prawns)

1 tsp sugar

2 tbsp light soy sauce

3 tbsp vegetable broth (stock)

Salt and pepper

Cilantro (coriander) leaves, to garnish

Method

Prep and cook time: 40 min

1. Cook the noodles in plenty of boiling, salted water according to the packet instructions and drain well.

2. Heat the oil in a wok or large skillet (frying pan), add the chicken and stir-fry for 2–3 minutes until golden brown.

3. Add the scallions, onions and garlic and fry for 3 minutes. Add the pak choi, chili, ginger and the shrimp (prawns) and fry for a further 2 minutes. Sprinkle over the sugar, soy sauce and stock and season with salt and pepper. Mix in the noodles and heat, stirring, until warm. Serve immediately.

VIETNAMESE MARINATED CHICKEN

Ingredients

4 tbsp light soy sauce

1 tsp tomato paste (purée)

4 chicken breasts, skinned and cut into bite size chunks

4 tbsp vegetable oil

1 onion, finely sliced

2 tsp sugar

6 scallions (spring onions), sliced

2 tbsp fish sauce

Juice of 1 lime

Salt and pepper

Fish sauce for dipping

Method

Prep and cook time: 20 min plus 30 min to marinate

1. Mix together the soy sauce and tomato paste (purée) and add the chicken. Set aside to marinate for 30 minutes.

2. Heat the oil in a wok or large skillet and fry the onions until they are lightly browned. Stir in the sugar and cook for 2 more minutes.

3. Add the chicken pieces and the marinade. Fry the chicken until it is cooked through then stir in the scallions (spring onions).

4. Stir briefly then pour over the fish sauce and lime juice. Season with salt and pepper and serve with fish sauce for dipping.

CHICKEN WITH RED PEPPERS

Ingredients

4 tbsp soy sauce

2 tbsp sherry

Thumb-size piece ginger, peeled and grated

4 chicken breasts, skinned and chopped into cubes

3 tbsp vegetable oil

2 garlic cloves, crushed

4 shallots, cut into wedges

2 red bell peppers, deseeded and cut into chunks

1 cup / 150 g cashew nuts

2 tbsp hoisin sauce

Method

Prep and cook time: 30 min plus
1 hour to marinate

1. Mix 2 tbsp of the soy sauce with the sherry and ginger and rub into the chicken pieces. Set aside to marinade for 1 hour.

2. Heat the vegetable oil in a wok until just smoking. Add the garlic, shallots, chicken and bell peppers and stir-fry for about 5 minutes or until the chicken is cooked through.

3. Add the cashew nuts, hoisin sauce and remaining soy sauce and fry briefly. Serve immediately on a bed of rice.

CHICKEN LASAGNE

Ingredients

12 sheets lasagne

2 tbsp olive oil

2 tbsp butter

1 onion, finely chopped

1 clove garlic, finely chopped

2 slices bacon, chopped

2 chicken breasts, skinned and chopped

1 zucchini (courgette), finely chopped

8 medium tomatoes, skinned, seeds removed and flesh chopped

1 cup / 100 g grated Parmesan cheese

Method

Prep and cook time: 45 min

1. Heat the oven to 375ºF (190ºC / Gas Mark 5).

2. Cook the lasagne sheets according to packet instructions and set aside.

3. Heat the oil and butter in a large pan and gently cook the onion until soft but not brown. Add the garlic and cook for 1 more minute then add the bacon and cook until the fat starts to run.

4. Add the chopped chicken, cook for 2 minutes then add the zucchini (courgette) and cook gently until the zucchini has softened. Stir in the tomatoes and season with salt and pepper.

5. Layer the lasagne sheets with the filling in an ovenproof dish, finishing with a layer of lasagne sheets. Sprinkle over the cheese and bake in the oven for 20–30 minutes or until the top is golden brown.

PASTA WITH CHICKEN AND BACON

Ingredients

3½ cups / 450 g trofie pasta

2 large tomatoes

Oil, for frying

1 chicken breast, cut into thin strips

4 oz / 100 g lean bacon, diced

1 onion, finely chopped

2 cups / 150 g mushrooms, sliced

Scant 1 cup / 100 g finely grated
Emmental or Cheddar cheese

Salt & freshly milled pepper

Method

Prep and cook time: 25 min

1. Cook the pasta in boiling, salted water
according to the instructions on the packet
until al dente.

2. Drop the tomatoes into boiling water for
a few seconds, refresh in cold water, then
skin, quarter, deseed and chop.

3. Heat the oil in a skillet and fry the
chicken for a few minutes. Add the bacon
and then the onion and the mushroom and
sauté for about 5 minutes. Now add the
tomatoes and the drained pasta and toss.

4. Remove the skillet from the heat and
season with salt and pepper. Fold in half the
cheese. Sprinkle the remaining cheese over
the top before serving.

SPAGHETTI WITH BACON, WALNUTS, AND GORGONZOLA

Ingredients

14 oz / 400 g spaghetti

1 onion, finely chopped

2 tbsp nut oil

1 chicken breast, cut into thin strips

2 oz / 50 g diced bacon

½ cup / 50 g shelled walnuts

Some fresh parsley, shredded

Salt & freshly milled pepper

4 oz / 100 g Gorgonzola cheese

Method

Prep and cook time: 25 min

1. Cook the spaghetti in boiling, salted water until al dente, then refresh in cold water and drain.

2. Heat the oil and fry the chicken for a few minutes. Add the onion and bacon and cook until golden brown. Add the walnuts, fry briefly. Check that the chicken is cooked through and then add the pasta and fry briefly.

3. Sprinkle over the shredded parsley and season with pepper and a little salt.

4. Crumble the Gorgonzola over the pasta and serve at once on plates or in bowls.

PENNE WITH CHICKEN, PEA AND LEMON SAUCE

Ingredients

2 chicken breasts, sliced into thin strips

1 shallot, finely chopped

1 garlic clove, finely chopped

2 tbsp butter

1 tbsp flour

$^2/_3$ cup / 150 ml chicken broth (stock)

$^1/_3$ cup / 80 ml whipping cream

Salt and freshly ground pepper

1 cup / 150 g frozen peas, thawed

1 lemon, zest and juice

1 lb / 450 g penne

1 tbsp finely chopped parsley

Method

Prep and cook time: 30 min

1. Sauté the chicken, shallot and garlic in hot butter. Sprinkle the flour on top. Mix and sauté briefly.

2. Add the broth (stock) and cream while stirring. Season with salt and pepper and bring to a boil. Add the peas and simmer over low heat for about 10 minutes. Stir occasionally.

3. Zest the lemon and squeeze out the juice.

4. Meanwhile, cook the penne in well-salted boiling water until al dente.

5. Add the parsley and lemon zest to the cream sauce. Season with a little lemon juice, salt and pepper.

6. Divide the well-drained pasta among the plates. Pour the sauce over the top and serve.

CHICKEN BREAST ON LINGUINE AND VEGETABLES

Ingredients

For the chicken:

2 chicken breasts, cut in half horizontally

3 tbsp vegetable oil

1 red chili pepper, deseeded and very finely chopped

1 tbsp lemon juice

Salt and pepper

For the linguine:

1 lb / 450 g linguine

4 tbsp olive oil

1 red onion, sliced

2 cloves garlic, finely chopped

2 red bell peppers, deseeded and sliced

1 cup / 75 g sliced button mushrooms

2 tbsp chopped parsley

Method

Prep and cook time: 50 min

1. Put the halved chicken breasts between 2 sheets of plastic wrap (cling film) and flatten with a rolling pin or meat tenderizer.

2. Mix together the vegetable oil, chopped chili and lemon juice and season with salt and pepper. Rub into the chicken pieces and set aside.

3. Bring a large pan of salted water to a boil and cook the linguine according to the packet instructions. Meanwhile, heat 3 tbsp the olive oil in a wide pan and gently cook the onion until it is beginning to soften.

4. Add the garlic and bell peppers to the pan, cook for 2 minutes then add the mushrooms. Cook gently, stirring from time to time, until the bell pepper and mushrooms are tender. Season with salt and pepper.

5. Heat the remaining oil in a large skillet and gently fry the chicken pieces for about 3 minutes on each side or until the chicken is cooked through.

6. Drain the linguine and stir through the bell pepper and mushroom mix. Place onto warmed serving plates, top with the cooked chicken and scatter over the parsley.

CHICKEN BREAST WITH TOMATO SAUCE

Ingredients

4 tbsp olive oil

1 onion, chopped

2 cloves garlic, chopped

14 oz / 400 g canned tomatoes

1 tbsp chopped thyme

1 tbsp chopped oregano

Salt and pepper

1 tbsp chopped parsley

4 chicken breast escalopes,
each about 100 g

½ cup / 125 ml white wine

7 oz / 200 g green beans

2 tbsp butter

7 oz / 200 g button mushrooms,
quartered

Method

Prep and cook time: 45 min

1. Heat 2 tbsp of the oil in a pan and gently cook the onion and garlic until soft but not browned. Add the tomatoes, thyme and oregano, season with salt and pepper and cook gently for 20–25 minutes, stirring from time to time, then stir in the parsley.

2. Meanwhile, heat the remaining oil in a wide pan and fry the chicken escalopes for 2 minutes on each side. Add the wine, let it bubble then turn the heat down and cook the chicken for a further 8 minutes, turning once, or until the chicken is cooked through. Remove the chicken from the pan and keep warm to rest.

3. While the chicken is cooking, boil the beans in salted water for 5 minutes then drain well.

4. While the chicken is resting, add the butter to the chicken pan and cook the mushrooms for 5 minutes until lightly browned and tender.

5. Serve the chicken with the tomato sauce and vegetables accompanied with pasta, if wished.

PAPPARDELLE WITH CHICKEN, OLIVES AND RED WINE SAUCE

Ingredients

2 tbsp oil

1 tbsp butter

4 oz / 100 g pancetta or bacon, chopped

1 clove garlic, crushed

1 red chili pepper, deseeded and chopped

2 large chicken breasts, skinned

6 oz / 150 g button mushrooms, whole

1 cup / 250 ml red wine

½ cup / 125 ml chicken broth (stock) or water

Salt and pepper

1 lb / 450 g pappardelle

1 cup / 100 g black olives

2 tbsp chopped parsley

Method

Prep and cook time: 45 min

1. Heat the oil and butter in a large pan and gently cook the pancetta or bacon until the fat starts to run.

2. Add the garlic and chili pepper, cook for 1 minute then add the chicken and cook for 3 minutes, pulling the meat apart as it begins to cook. Add the mushrooms then pour over the wine and chicken broth (stock).

3. Season with salt and pepper and simmer gently, stirring from time to time, until the chicken is cooked through.

4. Meanwhile, cook the pappardelle according to the packet instructions.

5. Turn the heat up on the chicken pan to reduce the sauce then stir in the olives and parsley.

6. Stir the pasta into the sauce, heat through and serve immediately.

PAPRIKA CHICKEN ON TAGLIATELLE

Ingredients

1 lb / 450 g tagliatelle

3 tbsp vegetable oil

1 onion, sliced

2 cloves garlic, finely chopped

2 tsp paprika

2 chicken breasts, skinned and cut into small chunks

1 red bell pepper, deseeded and chopped

1 green bell pepper, deseeded and chopped

1 yellow bell pepper, deseeded and chopped

2 tbsp sour cream

Salt and pepper

Chopped dill weed (dill), to garnish

Method

Prep and cook time: 30 min

1. Bring a large pan of salted water to a boil and cook the tagliatelle according to the packet instructions.

2. Heat the oil in a large skillet and gently cook the onion until soft but not brown. Add the garlic, cook for 1 more minute then stir in the paprika.

3. Add the chicken and cook for 5 minutes, stirring all the time, then add the chopped bell peppers and continue cooking until the chicken is cooked through.

4. Stir in the sour cream, season with salt and pepper and heat through. Serve on a bed of tagliatelle and garnish with the dill weed.

PASTA WITH SPINACH, TOMATOES AND CHICKEN

Ingredients

8 oz / 200 g stubby macaroni, such as penne, ziti or rigatoni

1 tbsp olive oil

1 skinless, boneless chicken breast, cubed

½ cup / 125 ml milk

½ cup / 125 ml light cream

½ cup / 150 g frozen spinach, thawed

2 tbsp instant flour (thickening granules)

1 tbsp grated Parmesan cheese

Salt and freshly ground pepper

8 cherry tomatoes, halved

4 basil leaves, to garnish

Method

Prep and cook time: 30 min

1. Bring a large pan of salted water to a boil. Add the macaroni and cook according to package instructions, until al dente.

2. Meanwhile, heat the oil in a large skillet. Add the chicken and fry, turning as needed, until cooked through, about 10 minutes.

3. Combine the milk, cream and spinach in a medium saucepan; stir in the instant flour (thickening granules), bring to a boil and simmer, stirring, until thickened. Stir in the Parmesan cheese and season with salt and pepper.

4. Drain the macaroni and add to the creamy sauce with the chicken and tomatoes.

6. Serve the pasta in bowls garnished with basil leaves.

CHICKEN BREAST WITH SPAGHETTI PUTTANESCA

Ingredients

1 lb / 400 g spaghetti

5 tbsp olive oil

2 cloves garlic, finely chopped

6 anchovy fillets, finely chopped

½ tsp dried chili flakes

1 tbsp chopped thyme

1 tbsp chopped rosemary

1 tbsp chopped parsley

1 tbsp chopped oregano

4 chicken breasts, skinned

2 tbsp / 30 g butter

1 lb / 400 g cherry tomatoes, halved

½ cup / 125 ml red wine

1 cup / 100 g black olives, roughly chopped

Method

Prep and cook time: 40 min

1. Heat the oven to 400°F (200°C / Gas Mark 6).

2. Cook the spaghetti according to the package instructions.

3. While the spaghetti is cooking, heat 4 tbsp of the oil in a large ovenproof skillet and gently fry the garlic, anchovies and chili flakes until softened but not brown.

4. Stir in the herbs then add the chicken breasts. Cook for 2 minutes then flip the chicken over and place in the oven for 10–15 minutes or until cooked through. When the chicken is cooked, remove the pan from the oven and keep warm.

5. While the chicken is cooking, heat the rest of the oil and the butter in a wide pan, add the tomatoes and cook very gently for 5 minutes. Pour over the wine, let bubble for 2 minutes then stir in the olives and season with salt and pepper.

6. When the spaghetti is cooked, drain well and stir into the tomato/olive mixture.

7. Serve the spaghetti with the chicken breasts and the herby meat juices poured over.

PASTA BAKE

Ingredients

2 eggs, separated

1 cup / 250 ml whipping cream

2 tbsp crème fraîche

Scant ½ cup / 50 g grated
Cheddar cheese

Salt and freshly milled pepper

Pinch nutmeg

4 oz / 250 g cooked chicken, diced

4 oz / 250 g cooked ham, diced

14 oz / 400 g ribbon pasta

1 tbsp soft butter

2 tbsp breadcrumbs

2 tbsp chopped fresh chives

Method

Prep and cook time: 1 hour

1. Mix the cream and the crème fraîche with the egg yolks until smooth.

2. Stir in the grated cheese and season with salt, pepper and nutmeg. Add the diced chicken and ham and mix well with the ribbon pasta. Whisk the egg whites until stiff, and then fold into the pasta.

3. Pre-heat the oven to 400°F (200°C / Gas Mark 6). Butter a baking dish and coat the base with breadcrumbs. Put the ribbon pasta mix in the dish and place in the oven for about 30 minutes until golden brown.

4. Sprinkle the chopped chives over the top and serve.

RIGATONI WITH CHICKEN AND BROCCOLI

Ingredients

4½ cups / 400 g rigatoni or tortiglioni

14 oz / 400 g grilled chicken

14oz / 400 g broccoli florets

1½ oz / 40 g sun-dried tomatoes

2 garlic cloves

4 tsp oil

1 lemon

2 tbsp black olives, chopped

Salt & freshly milled pepper

2–3 tbsp chopped parsley

Method

Prep and cook time: 30 min

1. Cook the pasta in plenty of boiling, salted water until al dente.

2. Meanwhile, remove the chicken meat from the bones and cut into pieces.

3. Blanch the broccoli in boiling, salted water for 3–4 minutes, then refresh in cold water and drain.

4. Chop the sun-dried tomatoes. Peel and crush the garlic. Heat the oil in a skillet and add the garlic, tomatoes and chicken. Season lightly with salt and pepper. Grate a little lemon zest into the pan, squeeze in lemon juice, to taste, and warm over a low heat for 8–10 minutes.

5. Add the broccoli and heat very gently for a further 5 minutes or so. Mix in the chopped olives and parsley and reheat.

6. Season to taste with salt and pepper. Then mix with the drained pasta and serve hot.

CHICKEN IN BASIL SAUCE

Ingredients

1 lb / 450 g green ribbon noodles

4 oz / 120 g shallots, finely chopped

1 lb 8 oz / 675g boneless chicken breasts, skinned and cubed

1 lb 12 oz / 800 g tomatoes

1 cup / 25 g basil leaves

3 tbsp vegetable oil

Scant 1 cup / 200 g crème fraîche

7 tbsp / 100 ml whipping cream

Salt and pepper

½ cup / 50 g Parmesan cheese, half grated, half sliced

Method
Prep and cook time: 40 min

1. Cook the noodles according to the package directions until tender but still with a slight bite. Drain well.

2. Blanch the tomatoes in boiling water, immerse in cold water and remove the skins. Coarsely chop the flesh.

3. Reserve a few of the basil leaves. Chop the rest into thin strips.

4. Heat the oil in a wok and fry the shallots until softened. Add the chicken and stir for about 1 minute.

5. Stir in the tomatoes, crème fraîche and cream. Add the basil and season with salt and pepper. Continue to fry over a high heat for 4 minutes, stirring continuously, until the chicken is cooked through.

6. Add the drained noodles and mix together. Garnish with slices of Parmesan cheese and the reserved basil leaves and serve the grated cheese separately for sprinkling on top.

CHICKEN AND MUSHROOM TAGLIATELLE

Ingredients

1 small onion

2 carrots

3 boneless chicken breasts, skinned

2 sprigs fresh thyme

1 cup / 225 ml water

2 tbsp dry sherry (optional)

Salt and pepper

1 lb / 450 g tagliatelle

9 oz / 250 g button mushrooms

2 garlic cloves

4 tbsp / 50 g butter

1 tbsp all-purpose (plain) white flour

Chopped fresh flat-leaf parsley,
to garnish

Method

Prep and cook time: 50 min

1. Cut the onion into quarters and the carrots into batons. Put in a large saucepan with the chicken, thyme, water and sherry, if using. Season generously with salt and pepper.

2. Bring to the boil, then reduce the heat and simmer for 15 minutes until the chicken is cooked through and tender when pierced with a fork. Add more water during cooking if necessary. Drain, set the chicken and vegetables aside and reserve the broth (stock).

3. Put the tagliatelle into a saucepan of boiling salted water and cook according to the packet instructions until tender but still with a slight bite.

4. Meanwhile, slice the mushrooms and crush the garlic. Melt the butter in a skillet (frying pan), add the mushrooms and garlic and fry for 5 minutes until softened.

5. Add the flour and cook for 1 minute. Gradually add the broth, stirring all the time, and cook until the sauce has thickened. Add the chicken and vegetables and heat through.

6. Drain the tagliatelle and divide between 4 serving plates. Put the chicken and mushroom mixture on top and serve sprinkled with parsley.

PENNE WITH POTATOES, CHICKEN AND GREEN BEANS

Ingredients

12 oz / 300 g small new potatoes

½ lb / 250–300 g green beans, trimmed and halved

2 small skinless boneless chicken breasts

Salt and freshly ground pepper

4 tbsp olive oil, divided

2½ cups / 300 g penne

1 tbsp finely chopped fresh basil

1 tbsp finely chopped fresh parsley

About 1 oz / 40 g Parmesan cheese

Method

Prep and cook time: 35 min

1. Scrub the potatoes and boil them in a large pan of salted water until cooked. Meanwhile, bring a saucepan of salted water to boil and add the beans and cook until tender-crisp, 8–10 minutes. Drain in a colander under cold running water to stop the cooking; set aside.

2. Season the chicken breasts with salt and pepper. Fry in 1 tablespoon of the oil for about 5 minutes on each side until cooked through, then remove from the skillet. Slice diagonally into strips and keep warm.

3. Cook the penne in boiling salted water until al dente; drain.

4. Meanwhile, heat the remaining oil in a large skillet. Halve the boiled potatoes and add them to the skillet along with the green beans and cook, stirring frequently. Season with salt and pepper. Combine with the penne and gently stir in the chicken strips, basil and parsley.

5. Arrange onto plates. Shave Parmesan cheese over the top and serve.

QUICK COUSCOUS WITH CHICKEN AND VEGETABLES

Ingredients

2 boneless skinless chicken breasts, chopped

2½ cups / 600 ml water

2 cups / 400 g frozen mixed vegetables,such as peas and carrots, sweetcorn

1⅓ cups / 200 g couscous

4 tbsp / 50 g butter

Method
Prep and cook time: 15 min

1. Place the chicken and water in a saucepan; bring to a boil, reduce heat and simmer for 5–8 minutes until the chicken is tender.

2. Add the frozen mixed vegetables and cook for 3 more minutes until the vegetables are tender and the chicken is cooked through.

3. Stir in the couscous, turn off the heat and let stand, covered, for a few minutes, until the liquid is absorbed.

4. Stir in the butter and serve.

JAMBALAYA

Ingredients

4 boneless chicken breasts, skinned

1 onion

1 celery stalk

2 garlic cloves

3 scallions (spring onions)

2 red bell peppers

2 red chilies

3 tbsp olive oil

1¼ cups / 250 g long grain rice

2 cups / 475 ml chicken broth (stock)

1 bay leaf

Salt and pepper

¾ cup / 150 g canned chopped tomatoes

2 tbsp chopped fresh cilantro (coriander) leaves

Ground cumin

Method
Prep and cook time: 50 min

1. Cut the chicken into slices. Chop the onion, celery and garlic. Slice the scallions (spring onions) into rings. Finely slice the red peppers and chilies, discarding the cores and seeds.

2. Heat the oil in a large skillet (frying pan), add the onion, garlic and scallions and fry for 2–3 minutes. Add the chicken and continue to fry for 1–2 minutes.

3. Stir in the celery, red pepper, chilies and rice. Pour in the chicken broth (stock) and add the bay leaf. Season with salt and pepper.

4. Cover the pan and simmer for about 20 minutes, stirring occasionally. When the rice is cooked, add the tomatoes and cilantro (coriander) leaves. Before serving, season to taste with cumin, salt and pepper.

CHICKEN AND RICE CASSEROLE

Ingredients

3 tbsp olive oil

3 chicken breasts, skinned

2 tbsp butter

2 leeks, chopped

2 cloves garlic, chopped

1½ cups / 300 g long-grain rice

1 cup / 250 ml white wine

2 cups / 500 ml chicken broth (stock)

½ bunch parsley, chopped

Method

Prep and cook time: 1 hour

1. Heat the oil in a deep skillet and cook the chicken breasts for about 4 minutes on each side or until cooked through and golden brown. Remove the meat from the pan and keep warm.

2. Heat the butter in the pan and gently cook the leeks and garlic until softened but not brown.

3. Add the rice, stir until coated then pour over the wine and chicken broth (stock). Bring to a boil then turn the heat down and let simmer gently, stirring from time to time, until the rice is tender and has absorbed the liquid. Add more water if necessary during cooking.

4. Cut the chicken pieces into chunks and stir into the rice with the chopped parsley. Season with salt and pepper and serve immediately.

CHICKEN WITH ZUCCHINI AND SPINACH ON RICE

Ingredients

2 tbsp sesame oil

2 chicken breasts, cut into strips

6 oz / 150 g tofu, sliced

2 zucchini (courgettes), sliced thinly lengthwise

2 cups / 150 g button mushrooms, thinly sliced

2 handfuls baby spinach

2 tbsp light soy sauce

Method

Prep and cook time: 30 min

1. Heat the oil in a wok or skillet until smoking and stir-fry the strips of chicken breasts for 2 minutes.

3. Add the tofu, zucchini (courgettes) and mushrooms and cook for 3 minutes or until the vegetables are just tender and the chicken is cooked through.

4. Add the baby spinach and cook until it wilts, then splash in the soy sauce.

5. Arrange the chicken, tofu, zucchini, mushrooms and spinach on a bed of rice.

CHICKEN TENDERS OVER SPANISH RICE

Ingredients

For the chicken:

4 chicken breasts, skinned and sliced in half horizontally

2 tbsp vegetable oil

2 tbsp honey

1 tbsp lemon juice

½ tsp paprika

Salt and pepper

For the rice:

2 tbsp vegetable oil

1 onion, chopped

1 clove garlic, chopped

1 green bell pepper, chopped

2 tomatoes, chopped

1 cup / 200 g rice

3 cups / 750 ml chicken broth (stock)

Method

Prep and cook time: 40 min

1. For the chicken, mix together the oil, honey and lemon juice. Season with salt and pepper and paprika and rub the mixture into the chicken pieces. Set aside to marinate while you cook the rice.

2. For the rice, heat the oil in a skillet and gently fry the onion until soft but not brown. Add the garlic, cook for 1 minute then stir in the bell pepper, tomatoes and the rice.

3. Cook for 2 minutes, stirring all the time then add the broth (stock). Bring to a boil, season with salt and pepper then turn the heat down and simmer for about 20 minutes or until the rice is cooked. You may need to add a little water during the cooking.

4. To cook the chicken, heat a griddle pan or broiler and broil the chicken pieces for about 3 minutes each side, turning once to make a criss-cross pattern, or until the chicken is cooked through. Serve with the Spanish rice with lettuce and tomato to garnish.

PAELLA

Ingredients

2 tomatoes

1 lb 12 oz / 800 g shellfish,
(e.g. mussels)

6 tbsp olive oil

About 2 lb / 1 kg of mixed skinless
and boneless chicken, cut into bite-
size pieces

1 onion, finely diced

1 clove garlic, finely diced

2 red bell peppers, cut into strips

Scant 1 cup / 100 g frozen peas

Salt & freshly milled pepper

1 cup / 200 g paella rice

1¾ cups / 400 ml chicken broth (stock)

1 bay leaf

4 saffron threads

Method
Prep and cook time: 1 hour

1. Drop the tomatoes into boiling water for
a few seconds, then skin, quarter, de-seed
and chop.

2. Scrub the shellfish, scrape off the 'beards'
from the mussels. Discard any shells that do
not close when tapped.

3. Heat the oil in a large skillet or paella
pan and slowly sauté the chicken on all
sides until golden brown. Add the onion
and fry briefly. Add the chopped garlic, bell
peppers, tomatoes and peas and fry briefly.
Season with salt and pepper.

4. Scatter the rice into the skillet and stir
in carefully. Add the broth (stock), bay leaf
and the saffron dissolved in a little water.
You should not stir the paella again. Turn
down the heat and simmer without a lid for
25–30 minutes.

5. About 10 minutes before the end of
cooking time add the seafood. When
cooked, discard any shells that remain
closed. Check the seasoning and serve.
The liquid should have been absorbed.

CHICKEN AND ASPARAGUS RISOTTO

Ingredients

1 lb / 450 g asparagus

1 garlic clove

5 tbsp olive oil

4 boneless chicken breasts, skinned

Salt and pepper

¾ cup / 150 g risotto rice

2 cups / 475 ml vegetable broth (stock)

1 tbsp / 15 g butter

½ cup / 50 g freshly grated
Parmesan cheese

1 tbsp fresh thyme leaves

Method

Prep and cook time: 55 min

1. Peel the bottom third from the asparagus stalks and cut the spears into bite-size pieces. Crush the garlic.

2. Heat 2 tbsp oil in a large skillet (frying pan), add the garlic and fry for 30 seconds. Add the asparagus, fry for 1–2 minutes, then add a little water and cook very gently until tender but still with a slight bite. Remove from the skillet and set aside.

3. Cut the chicken breasts into cubes. Heat 2 tbsp of oil in the skillet, add the chicken pieces and fry until browned on all sides and cooked through. Season with salt and pepper and remove from the pan.

4. Heat the remaining 1 tbsp of oil in the pan. Add the rice and stir until slightly translucent, then add a ladleful of broth (stock) and stir until it has been absorbed. Continue in this way, gradually adding more broth and stirring all the time, until the rice is tender but still has a slight bite and the risotto is creamy. This will take about 20 minutes.

5. Stir in the chicken and asparagus and add the butter and grated Parmesan cheese. Season to taste with salt and pepper, stir in the thyme leaves and serve.

PAN-COOKED CHICKEN WITH RICE

Ingredients

1 cup / 200 g long grain rice

3½ cups / 900 ml vegetable broth (stock)

4 chicken legs, with skin on

Salt

2 green bell peppers

4 tomatoes

14 oz / 400 g frozen peas

2 tbsp paprika

1–2 tsp cayenne pepper

Method

Prep and cook time: 1 hour

1. Preheat the oven to 325°F (170°C / Gas Mark 3).

2. Wash and drain the rice. Put into a saucepan with 2½ cups / 600 ml of the vegetable broth (stock), bring to the boil and simmer for about 20 minutes until tender.

3. Season the chicken legs with salt, put into an ovenproof dish, and add the remaining vegetable broth. Cook the chicken in the oven for 20 minutes.

4. Meanwhile, roughly dice the green peppers, discarding the cores and seeds. Cut the tomatoes in half and dice the flesh, discarding the seeds. Add the peas, peppers and tomatoes to the rice and season with salt.

5. Remove the chicken legs from the baking dish. Put the rice and vegetables into the dish and mix with the meat juices. Place the chicken legs, skin side up,on top of the rice and sprinkle with paprika and cayenne pepper.

6. Return to the oven and cook for a further 15 minutes until the chicken legs are golden brown and cooked through.

CHICKEN CREOLE

Ingredients

Serves 6

2 tbsp oil

1 onion, chopped

2 garlic cloves, chopped

1 stick celery, chopped

1 lb / 450 g skinless boneless chicken

8 oz / 225 g smoked sausage, sliced

2 cups / 450 g long-grain rice

1 bay leaf

1 tsp chopped thyme

1 tsp chopped oregano

1 tbsp Cajun seasoning

15 oz / 400 g can tomatoes

2 cups / 500 ml water

1 tsp salt

2 tbsp chopped cilantro (coriander)

Method

Prep and cook time: 35 min

1. Heat 1 tbsp oil in a heavy pan and fry the onion, garlic and celery until the onion starts to color and soften.

2. Add the chicken and sausage and fry until the chicken is browned.

3. Put another 1 tbsp of oil into the pan. Add the rice, spices and herbs, then stir well to ensure the rice is well coated.

4. Add the tomatoes, the water and the salt. Cover the pan and bring to a boil. Simmer gently for about 15–20 minutes or until the rice is cooked. Stir once or twice during cooking. Serve garnished with the chopped cilantro (coriander).

CHICKEN BURGERS

Ingredients

3 tbsp vegetable oil

1 small onion, finely chopped

1 clove garlic, finely chopped

1 green chili pepper, deseeded and finely chopped

1 lb / 450 g ground (minced) chicken

2 tbsp chopped parsley

1 tbsp chopped cilantro (fresh coriander)

2 cups / 100 g breadcrumbs

Salt and pepper

2 eggs

1 cup / 100 g flour

Vegetable oil, for frying

Method

Prep and cook time: 30 min

1. Heat the oil in a skillet and gently fry the onion until soft but not brown. Add the garlic and chili and cook for a further 2 minutes.

2. Add the chicken and fry briefly then transfer to a mixing bowl and add half a cup of breadcrumbs and the herbs. Season with salt and pepper and mix in one of the eggs.

3. Beat the remaining egg and place in a shallow dish. Season the flour with salt and pepper and place in another shallow dish.

4. Shape the chicken into patty shapes, dredge in the seasoned flour, dip into the beaten egg then roll in the remaining breadcrumbs.

5. Heat the oil in a deep pan and fry the patties for about 6 minutes or until they are golden brown and crisp and the chicken is cooked through. Drain on kitchen paper and serve.

CHICKEN KIEV

Ingredients

4 chicken breasts, skinned

1 bunch parsley, chopped

5 tbsp / 75 g butter, softened

2 cloves garlic, crushed

Salt and pepper

½ cup / 50 g flour

2 eggs, beaten

1 cup / 50 g breadcrumbs

Oil, for deep frying

String beans, to serve

Baby spinach, to serve

Method

Prep and cook time: 30 min

1. Make horizontal slits in each chicken breast to make a pocket.

2. Mix together the parsley, butter and garlic, season with salt and pepper, and stuff into the pockets in the chicken.

3. Season the flour with salt and pepper and place in a shallow dish. Dust the chicken breasts with the flour, dip them into the beaten eggs and coat them in the breadcrumbs. Dip them into the eggs once again and then give then a final coat of breadcrumbs.

4. Heat the oil in a deep pan until smoking then deep fry the chicken for about 10 minutes or until golden brown and cooked through.

5. Serve immediately with string beans and baby spinach.

KOFTA CURRY

Ingredients

For the sauce:

3 tbsp oil

1 onion, chopped

2 garlic cloves, chopped

Thumb-size piece ginger, finely chopped

1 tsp each of: curcuma (turmeric), chili powder, paprika, ground cinnamon and ground coriander

2 cups / 400 g canned tomatoes

1 cup / 250 ml vegetable broth (stock)

Salt and pepper

For the kofta:

1 onion, roughly chopped

2 garlic cloves, chopped

2 tbsp chopped cilantro (coriander)

2 tbsp chopped parsley

1 tsp ground cinnamon

1 lb / 450 g ground (minced) chicken

1 egg, beaten

4 tbsp oil

For the batter:

4 eggs

50 g / ½ cup flour

1 tsp baking powder

1 tsp salt

Oil, for deep frying

To serve:

12 cherry tomatoes, quartered

Chopped parsley

Method

Prep and cook time: 1 hour

1. For the sauce, heat the oil in a deep pan and gently cook the onion until soft but not brown.

2. Add the garlic, ginger and all the spices and cook for 2 minutes, stirring all the time.

3. Pour in the tomatoes and vegetable broth (stock), season with salt and pepper and simmer gently for 15 minutes.

4. Blend the sauce to a purée, pass through a fine sieve and keep warm.

5. For the koftas, put the onion, garlic, cilantro (coriander) and parsley in a food processor and blend to make a paste.

6. Mix the paste with the chicken and beaten egg, season with salt and pepper and roll into balls.

7. Heat the oil in a skillet and fry the koftas for 5 minutes making sure they are evenly cooked.

8. Beat the batter ingredients together with half a cup of warm water. Heat the oil in a deep pan until bubbles appear on a wooden spoon held in the oil. Dip the koftas into the batter and deep fry in batches until golden brown. Drain on kitchen paper.

9. Serve the koftas in the sauce with the cherry tomatoes and parsley scattered over.

CHICKEN TONKATSU IN SOY SAUCE

Ingredients

4 chicken breasts, skinned

4 tbsp all purpose (plain) flour

Salt and pepper

2 eggs, beaten

2 cups / 150 g panko breadcrumbs

1 cup / 250 ml vegetable oil

Soy sauce, to serve

Method

Prep and cook time: 20 min

1. Put the chicken breasts between two sheets of plastic wrap (clingfilm) and bash with a rolling pan to flatten.

2. Season the flour with salt and pepper and place in a shallow bowl.

3. Place the beaten eggs in a shallow bowl and the breadcrumbs onto a plate.

4. Heat the oil in a large skillet over a medium heat.

5. Dip the chicken breasts in the flour, shake off any excess then dip into the egg and then the breadcrumbs.

6. Fry the chicken for 3–4 minutes on each side or until golden brown and cooked through. Drain on kitchen paper, cut into slices and serve hot, dipping in the soy sauce.

CARIBBEAN COCONUT CHICKEN NUGGETS

Ingredients

4 chicken breasts, skinned

$^2/_3$ cup / 75 g flour

Salt and pepper

1 tsp paprika

1 cup / 75 g panko breadcrumbs

1 cup / 75 g desiccated coconut

2 eggs, beaten

Vegetable oil, for deep frying

Method

Prep and cook time: 30 min

1. Cut the chicken into bite size chunks.

2. Season the flour with salt, pepper and paprika and place into a shallow dish. Mix the breadcrumbs and coconut together and place in a shallow bowl.

3. Dust the chicken pieces with the seasoned flour, dip into the beaten egg and then into the breadcrumb and coconut mix, making sure they are thoroughly coated.

4. Heat the oil in a deep pan until smoking then deep fry the chicken pieces for about 5 minutes or until golden brown and cooked through. Drain on kitchen paper and serve immediately.

CHICKEN BALLS

Ingredients

3 slices day-old white bread

Generous ¾ cup / 200 ml whipping cream

1 tbsp chopped scallions (spring onions), plus extra to garnish

1 lb 8 oz / 650 g ground (minced) chicken

3 tbsp lemon juice

2 tbsp chopped fresh lemon balm or lemon thyme

2 tbsp chopped fresh mint

Salt and pepper

6 tbsp fresh breadcrumbs

2 tbsp sesame seeds

4 tbsp vegetable oil

Carrot ribbons, to garnish

Method

Prep and cook time: 30 min

1. Tear the bread into small pieces and put in a large bowl. Add the cream and leave until softened.

2. Add the scallions (spring onions) to the bread with the chicken, lemon juice, lemon balm or thyme and the mint, and mix together. Season with salt and pepper.

3. With damp hands, form the meat mixture into balls. You should make about 20.

4. Put the breadcrumbs and sesame seeds in a shallow dish and mix together. Coat the chicken balls in the mixture.

5. Heat the oil in a skillet (frying pan), add the chicken balls and fry for about 5 minutes, browning all sides until thoroughly cooked through. Serve garnished with the scallions and carrot ribbons.

BAKED CHICKEN AND BROCCOLI RISOTTO

Ingredients

2 tbsp / 25 g butter

1 onion, chopped

12 oz / 300 g risotto rice

½ cup / 150 g broccoli, cut into small florets

5 oz / 150 g cooked chicken, shredded

3 cups / 700 ml hot vegetable broth (stock)

½ cup / 50 g Cheddar cheese, grated

1 oz / 25 g plain dry breadcrumbs

Method

Prep and cook time: 35 min

1. Heat the oven to 400F (200C / Gas Mark 6).

2. Heat the butter in a flameproof casserole. Add the onion and cook, stirring, for 3–4 minutes until softened but not browned.

3. Stir in the rice and mix well until coated. Add the broccoli, chicken and the hot broth (stock), then give the rice a quick stir.

4. Cover with a tightly fitting lid and bake for 15–20 minutes until the rice is just cooked.

5. Stir in the cheese and sprinkle with the breadcrumbs. Return to the oven for a few minutes until the crumb topping is golden.

CHICKEN, POTATO AND CHEESE BAKE

Ingredients

$^2/_3$ cup / 150 ml milk

$^2/_3$ cups / 150 ml heavy (double) cream

1 lb / 450 g even-sized small potatoes, thinly sliced

6 oz / 180 g cooked chicken

1 tsp / 15 g butter, chopped

½ cup / 100 g grated Cheddar cheese

½ tsp thyme leaves

Method

Prep and cook time: 1 h 20 min

1. Heat the oven to 400F (200C / Gas Mark 6).

2. Whisk the milk and cream in a medium bowl. Grease a 750 ml / 3-cup baking dish.

3. Arrange a layer of sliced potatoes over the base of the dish, sprinkle with a little chicken, butter and cheese. Continue layering, alternating the potatoes with the chicken, butter and cheese. Pour over the milk and cream mixture and scatter over the thyme leaves.

4. Cover with foil and bake for 1 hour until the potatoes are tender. Remove the foil and cook for10 more minutes, until the topping is golden.

MEXICAN CHICKEN AND CHEESE PIE

Ingredients

3 cups / 300 g all-purpose (plain) flour

1 tbsp butter

1 tsp baking powder

½ tsp salt

½ cup / 125 ml boiling water

2 tbsp vegetable oil, plus some for greasing

2 onions, finely chopped

2 cloves garlic, finely chopped

2 green chili peppers, deseeded and finely chopped

4 eggs, beaten

4 handfuls spinach, wilted and chopped

2 chicken breasts, cooked and chopped

4 tbsp chopped cilantro (fresh coriander)

Salt and pepper

2 cups / 200 g grated cheese

Method

Prep and cook time: 1 hour

1. Heat the oven to 350°F (180°C /Gas Mark 4).

2. Place the flour in a bowl and rub in the butter until the mixture resembles fine breadcrumbs. Add the baking powder and salt and stir in just enough boiling water to make a dough. Turn onto a floured board and knead for 5 minutes then set aside in an oiled bowl while you make the filling.

3. Heat the oil in a pan and gently cook the onion until soft but not brown. Add the garlic and the chili peppers and cook for 2 more minutes then remove the pan from the heat.

4. Roll out the dough on a floured surface as thinly as possible and line a greased deep pie dish about 8 inch / 20 cm diameter.

5. Mix the onion mixture into the beaten eggs with the spinach, chicken and cilantro (coriander). Season with salt and pepper and pour into the pie dish.

6. Scatter over the cheese and bake in the oven for 30–40 minutes or until golden brown. Let cool a little in the pie dish before turning out. Serve warm or cold.

CHICKEN AND LEEK COBBLER

Ingredients

2 tbsp diced bacon

1 lb 8 oz / 650 g leeks

1 carrot

2 garlic cloves

2 large boneless chicken breasts, skinned

8 oz / 225 g ready-rolled puff pastry, thawed if frozen

Flour, for dusting

3 tbsp vegetable oil

5 tbsp dry white wine

2 cups / 475 ml chicken broth (stock)

Salt and pepper

Egg yolk, for glazing

Method

Prep and cook time: 45 min

1. Preheat the oven to 400°F (200°C / Gas Mark 6). Put the bacon in a skillet (frying pan) and fry in its own fat until browned. Leave to cool.

2. Meanwhile, thinly slice the leeks and carrot. Finely chop the garlic. Cut the chicken into bite-size pieces.

3. Sprinkle half the pastry sheets with the fried bacon and lay the other sheets on top. On a lightly floured surface, roll out to a thickness of ½ inch / 1 cm. Using a 2 inch / 5 cm cutter, cut out rounds.

4. Heat the oil in an ovenproof skillet and fry the garlic until softened. Add the chicken and brown on all sides. Add the leeks and carrot and fry for 1–2 minutes. Add the wine and cook until it has evaporated. Add the broth (stock) and season with salt and pepper.

5. Arrange the puff pastry rounds on top of the stew and brush with egg yolk.

6. Bake in the oven for 10–15 minutes until risen and golden brown.

CHICKEN AND PARSNIP PIES

Ingredients

1 lb / 450 g parsnips, peeled and quartered

½ lb / 250 g potatoes, peeled and chopped

1 tbsp olive oil

12 oz / 350 g skinless, boneless chicken breast, cut into chunks

1 small leek, trimmed and finely chopped (white part only)

½ cup / 100 g finely chopped carrot

²/₃ cup / 150 ml heavy (double cream)

2 tbsp / 25 g butter

2 tbsp milk

Method

Prep and cook time: 1 hour

1. Heat the oven to 400F (200C / Gas Mark 6).

2. Put the parsnips and potatoes together in a large saucepan with enough salted water to cover. Bring to a boil, reduce the heat and simmer for 20 minutes until tender.

3. Meanwhile, heat the oil in a large skillet (frying pan); add the chicken and fry for 5 minutes. Add the leek and cook for 5 more minutes.

4. Stir in the carrot and cream and warm through. Cook, stirring, until sauce thickens slightly.

5. Drain the potatoes and parsnips; return to the pan and mash until smooth. Beat in the butter and milk.

6. Divide the chicken mixture between 4 individual ovenproof dishes and top each one with one quarter of the potato mixture. Bake for 30 minutes until golden.

PASTILLA
(MOROCCAN CHICKEN PIE)

Ingredients

4 tbsp vegetable oil

2 large chicken legs, jointed

2 onions, chopped

1 clove garlic, crushed

Thumb-size piece fresh ginger, peeled and chopped

Pinch saffron threads

1 tsp ground ginger

1 tsp cinnamon

1 tsp paprika

2 tbsp chopped cilantro (fresh coriander)

2 tbsp parsley

1 cup / 100 g chopped almonds

1 tbsp sugar

Salt and pepper

7 tbsp / 100 g butter, melted

1 lb / 450 g filo pastry

Method

Prep and cook time: 1 hour 20 min

1. Heat the oil in a large pan and brown the chicken pieces on all sides. Remove the chicken from the pan.

2. Gently fry the onions in the pan until soft then add the garlic, ginger, saffron, cinnamon and paprika. Pour in just enough water to cover the chicken, add the cilantro and parsley and simmer gently for 30–40 minutes or until the chicken is cooked through.

3. Heat the oven to 400°F (200°C / Gas Mark 6). Remove the chicken from the pan and simmer the sauce until it is thick. Season with salt and pepper.

4. Lightly toast the almonds in a dry pan then stir in the sugar and add to the sauce.

5. Remove the meat from the chicken pieces, roughly chop and add to the sauce.

6. Brush a 9 inch / 24 cm springform cake pan with melted butter and line with overlapping sheets of filo pastry, brushing each sheet with melted butter as you go. The pastry sheets should hang over the sides of the pan.

7. Fill the pan with the chicken mixture, loosely drape the pastry over the top and bake in the oven for 20–30 minutes or until golden brown.

CHICKEN AND HAM PIE

Ingredients

1 lb / 450 g boneless chicken breasts, skinned

1¼ cups / 300 ml chicken broth (stock)

8 oz / 225 g cooked ham

1 shallot

4 tbsp / 50 g butter

2 tbsp all-purpose (plain) flour

²/₃ cup / 150 g crème fraîche

2 tbsp lemon juice

2 egg yolks

3 tbsp grated Cheddar cheese

2 tbsp finely chopped fresh parsley

Freshly grated nutmeg

Salt and pepper

For the pastry:

2 cups / 200 g all-purpose (plain) flour

1 tsp salt

5 tbsp / 70 g cold butter

5 tbsp / 70 g shortening or lard

1–2 tbsp ice-cold water

Flour, for dusting

Method

Prep and cook time: 1 hour 40 min

1. To make the pastry, put the flour and salt into a large bowl. Add the butter and shortening or lard, in small pieces, and rub in with your fingertips until the mixture forms breadcrumbs. Add enough ice-cold water to form a dough. Wrap in plastic wrap (cling film) and put into the refrigerator while you make the filling.

2. Preheat the oven to 400°F (200°C / Gas Mark 6). Cut the chicken into small, bite-size cubes. Put the broth (stock) into a saucepan and bring to the boil. Add the chicken and cook for 4–5 minutes. Remove from the pan with a slotted spoon, reserving the broth.

3. Cut the ham into small cubes, discarding any fat. Finely chop the shallot. Melt 1 tbsp / 15 g butter in a saucepan. Add the shallot and fry until translucent. Add the ham and fry for about 3 minutes then remove from the heat.

4. Heat the remaining butter in a separate pan. Add the flour and stir until it has absorbed the fat. Gradually stir in the broth, bring to the boil, stirring, and then remove from the heat.

5. Put the crème fraîche, lemon juice and 1 egg yolk in a bowl and mix together. Stir into the sauce with the cheese. Add the chicken, ham and parsley and mix well together. Season with nutmeg, salt and pepper.

6. Divide the pastry in half and roll out each half on a floured surface into a round large enough to fit a 9 inch (23 cm) ovenproof pie dish.

7. Put 1 round in the base of the dish and spoon over the chicken filling. Place the second round on top and press the edges together to seal.

8. Beat the remaining egg yolk and brush on top to glaze. Bake in the oven for about 40 minutes until golden brown.

MEXICAN CHICKEN PANCAKES

Ingredients

Butter, for greasing

8 oz / 225 g cooked chicken

¼–½ tsp chili powder (optional)

1 bunch scallions (spring onions)

1¼ cups / 125 g all-purpose (plain) flour

2 eggs

Salt and pepper

²/₃ cup / 200 ml milk

2 tbsp vegetable oil

²/₃ cup / 200 ml sour (soured) cream

8 tbsp grated Cheddar cheese

Cilantro (coriander) leaves, to garnish

Method
Prep and cook time: 1 hour

1. Preheat the oven to 400°F (200°C / Gas Mark 6). Lightly butter 4 individual or 1 large ovenproof serving dish.

2. Cut the chicken into small pieces. Sprinkle the chicken with a little chili powder, if desired. Roughly chop the scallions (spring onions).

3. Put the flour and eggs into a large bowl and season with salt and pepper. Gradually beat in the milk to make a smooth batter.

4. Heat 1 tbsp of the oil in a skillet (frying pan). Add a ladleful of the batter and tip to cover the base of the pan. Cook for 1–2 minutes until the base is firm then flip and cook for a further 1 minute.

5. Repeat, using the remaining batter, to make 8 pancakes, interleaving the cooked pancakes with parchment paper.

6. Pour the sour cream into the base of the prepared dish or dishes. Sprinkle over the chopped scallions.

7. Place an eighth of the chicken pieces into the center of each pancake and add a little grated cheese to each, reserving a little to garnish.

8. Fold up each pancake, securing with a toothpick (cocktail stick), if needed. Carefully lift the pancakes on top of the sour cream mixture, allowing 2 per serving.

9. Bake in the oven for 15 minutes to warm through. Sprinkle the remaining cheese on top of each pancake and serve garnished with fresh cilantro (coriander) leaves.

CHICKEN ROULADES WITH CHEESE FILLING

Ingredients

4 chicken breasts, skinned

8 oz / 200 g cheese, Brie or similar

8 slices bacon

12 oz / 300 g cherry tomatoes,
on the vine

1 tsp balsamic vinegar

1 tbsp oil

Method

Prep and cook time: 50 min

1. Heat the oven to 400°F (200°C / Gas Mark 6).

2. Place each chicken breast between 2 pieces of plastic wrap (cling film) and bash with a rolling pin to flatten.

3. Season each chicken breasts with salt and pepper, slice the Brie and arrange the slices on top of the chicken breasts. Fold in the sides of the meat and roll up firmly.

4. Wrap each roulade in 2 slices of bacon and place in an oiled baking dish. Put into the preheated oven and cook for about 30 minutes.

5. Meanwhile, put the tomatoes into the baking dish with the roulades, sprinkle with balsamic vinegar and cook for a further 10 minutes.

FRITTATA WITH POTATO, PEA AND CHICKEN

Ingredients

1½ lb / 675 g waxy potatoes

6 eggs

3 tbsp whipping cream

Nutmeg

1 onion, sliced

2 tbsp olive oil

4 oz / 100 g cooked chicken, shredded

²/₃ cup / 100 g frozen peas

1 cup / 20 g baby spinach leaves, rinsed and coarsely chopped

1 tbsp chopped fresh basil

Salt and freshly ground pepper

Method

Prep and cook time: 45 min

1. Preheat the oven to 425 F (220C / Gas Mark 7).

2. Boil the potatoes in salted water for about 30 minutes or until they can be easily pierced with a knife. Allow to cool. Peel and cut into bite-size pieces.

4 Whisk the eggs with the cream. Season with salt, pepper and nutmeg.

5. Sauté the onion slices in hot oil. Add the potatoes and continue to sauté until golden brown, about 2–3 minutes.

6. Add the chicken, peas, spinach and basil. Pour in the eggs. Cook briefly, then place in the preheated oven for about 8 minutes until set.

INDEX